WHAT THE SPIRIT SAYS
TO THE CHURCHES

What the Spirit says to the Churches

A Key to the Apocalypse of John

by HUBERT J. RICHARDS

P. J. KENEDY & SONS—NEW YORK

Nihil obstat: Joannes M. T. Barton S.T.D., L.S.S.
          Censor deputatus
Imprimatur: ✠ Patritius Casey Vic. Gen.
Westmonasterii, die 26a Aprilis, 1966

The Nihil obstat and Imprimatur are a declaration that a book or pamphlet is considered to be free from doctrinal and moral error. It is not implied that those who have granted the Nihil obstat and Imprimatur agree with the contents, opinions or statements expressed.

Made and printed in Great Britain

To my father on earth
who first taught me
what it means to speak of
a Father in heaven

CONTENTS

I INTRODUCTION

Apart from a few stock quotations, the Apocalypse is probably the least read book of the whole Bible. Certainly it is the most neglected book of the New Testament. The reason for this is obvious enough. From its opening words it presents the reader with a series of brilliant and highly coloured visions which weave in and out of each other as in some fantastic nightmare. The two witnesses, the four horsemen, the seven trumpets, the thousand years, the hundred and forty-four thousand marked with a seal, the Harlot, the Beast and its mystic number, the Woman clothed with the sun and crowned with the stars ... what is he supposed to make of it all? Is there any real clue to the meaning of these things? And even if he can be satisfied that this vision refers to such an event and that vision to another, is there any earthly use to which he can put this information? How is it supposed to nourish him, spiritually?

He may even feel some sympathy for the saying that the Apocalypse is a book which either finds a man cracked or leaves him so, in other words that a person must be mad to try and find out what it is all about; if he is not, he will be mad when he has finished. Indeed there are good grounds for the saying; of all the strange literary forms to be found in the Bible, that of the Apocalypse is probably the most unusual and the furthest removed from the mentality of a man living in the twentieth century. But the reader should also know that if only he will make an effort to understand the book, there is a blessing waiting for him. In his very first paragraph the author goes on record with this statement:

> Blessed is he who reads and those who hear the words of this prophecy.

It is out of a conviction that these words are something more than an empty promise that the following chapters have been written.

Apocalypses in General

It may seem strange to speak of 'apocalypses' in the plural. It would have seemed even stranger a hundred years ago, when the book we are discussing was still the only apocalypse known, and stood in a class apart from any other literature. This made it the happy hunting ground for any scholar who was slightly eccentric. He could interpret the book exactly as he pleased and entirely on its own merits, because there was nothing else to compare it to or to check it by. It became quite common to read into the Apocalypse a reference to every event from the first century A.D. down to the present time, and to make of it a sort of *Old Moore's Almanac* giving a detailed prediction of all that was to happen until the end of the world. People could interpret the famous Beast in ch. 13 of anyone for whom they felt a dislike—Nero, Domitian, Mahomet, Luther, the Pope,*

---

* For instance an annotated Bible, published in London in 1613, has this comment to make on Apoc. 13[16-18]: 'This Antichrist will accept none but such as will aprove his doctrines: so that it is not enough to confesse Christ and to beleeve the Scriptures, but a man must subscribe to the Pope's doctrine: moreover their chrismatories, greasings, vowes, othes, and shavings are signes of this marke, insomuch as no nation was accepted that had not many of these marked beastes . . . About 666 years after this revelation the Pope or Antichrist began to be manifested in the world . . . This number is gathered from . . . $\lambda\alpha\tau\varepsilon\iota\nu o\varsigma$ . . . which noteth the Pope or Antichrist, who useth in alle things the Latine tongue, and in respect thereof hee contemneth the Hebrew and Greeke, wherein the word of God was first and best written . . . The Italians are called Latini, so that hereby he noteth of what countrey chiefley hee should come.' And on 17[3]: 'The beaste signifieth the ancient Rome: the woman that sitteth thereon, the new Rome, which is the Papistry, whose crueltie and bloodshedding is declared by scarlet. . . . This woman is the Pope with the whole body of his filthy creatures . . . whose beauty only standeth in outward pompe and impudencie, and craft like a strumpet.'

Napoleon—and there was nothing to stop them. Indeed the same kind of interpretation is still in vogue among the latter day prophets who almost daily interrupt the late night pops on Radio Luxembourg to read signs of the end in the history of our times, and who with a fine disregard for the research of scholars in the last hundred years have continued to identify the Beast with Kaiser Wilhelm, Hitler, Stalin and Mao Tse-tung

But St John's is not the only apocalypse. Within the last century dozens of apocalypses have been discovered and interpreted, and provided us at last with a gauge by which our book may be measured. The four hundred years between 200 B.C. and A.D. 200 saw the publication of a great number of works written in exactly the same style. The Book of Henoch, the fourth Book of Esdras, the Assumption of Moses, the Apocalypse of Baruch and the Psalms of Solomon are the most well known examples of this apocalyptic literature.*

Apokalypsai is a Greek word meaning to unveil or reveal. These books were known as 'apocalypses' because they claimed to lift the veil from what had so far remained hidden, to reveal what until now had been God's secret. In what sense did they claim to do this?

Apocalypse is prophecy in a new idiom. The prophetical movement, which had blossomed in the early days of Israel's monarchy and had borne as its fruit the unforgettable preaching of Amos, Hosea, Isaiah, Jeremiah and Ezekiel, entered into a slow decline from the moment that Israel was exiled to Babylonia in 600 B.C.—it produced no more great names after Ezekiel—and barely survived the journey back to Palestine a century later. By the year 300 B.C. it was dead. But the message it had preached was far from dead. It is true that the hopes which the prophets had always held out, of God's final intervention to destroy the forces of evil and establish his Kingdom on earth, seemed less and less likely of finding fulfilment as the

---

* It is interesting that the recently discovered literature of the Dead Sea Sect, itself composed during these centuries, contains more than one example of this same kind of writing.

years dragged on, and there were those who, seeing that Babylonian domination only gave way to Persian, and Persian to Greek, and Greek to Roman, were willing to abandon the prophetical hope entirely and turn to political means of restoring Israel's independence. But there were others who clung to the prophetical promise that God would one day show his hand, and they were determined to reassert that promise in a more and more striking form each time it seemed to be disappointed.

The form it took was apocalypse. If it was no longer sufficient to repeat God's constant promise of final victory, then that promise would be backed up by recalling the past victories in which God had already shown his hand to those who had eyes to see. And if it was no longer sufficient to look back on those victories in the past tense as part of history, then they would be put into a dramatic future tense, as if they were foretold long before they happened. The apparently hopeless future was as much under God's control as the past. To present both as foreordained by God was the most powerful plea to the reader to project his confidence in God's management of the first half (which he had already seen) into the second half (which he had not yet seen).

A typical example of this attempt to keep alive the message of the prophets may be seen in the book of Daniel. Written in the Maccabean age of the second century B.C., it takes a fictitious standpoint in the Babylonian exile four hundred years earlier, and describes the whole of Israel's history down to the author's own day as if it had been foretold to the Daniel who served in Nebuchadnezzar's court, with instructions to 'seal' the book in which he had written these prophecies until they were needed by the persecuted Maccabees. The reader picking this up in 170 B.C. would indeed be given the impression that he had come across an 'apocalypse', a revelation of something that had been hidden until now. But he was not fooled into thinking that he really was reading an ancient foretelling of the present. He knew that he was only seeing the future glory of Israel from a new standpoint, as part of a sequence and no longer in isolation. He knew that he was only being invited to walk back and look along the whole length of the line on which he had been working, so that he could see how straight it was.

The book of Daniel was only the first of a long series of books of this kind. All of them use the same technique of writing history 'forwards instead of backwards' to give their reader the confidence they needed in a time of stress and temptation to despair or apostasy.* All of them support their hope of future glory on the detailed history of the past and present already known to the reader. All of them depend for their effect on being the written rather than the spoken word, and they were issued either anonymously or under a pseudonym; the whole literary form demanded that the impression be given of a revelation made long ago, and the direct preaching of it would have ruined this fiction on which its impact depended. For the same reason all of them were deliberately obscure, not simply to arouse the curiosity of those for whom the message was meant and to hide it from those for whom it was not meant (though no doubt these aspects had their part to play, as they have done in any resistance literature), but primarily to give the message a chance of looking like the vague and apparently unintelligible picture of the distant future that it was meant to be, and not too much like the back-to-front history that it was.

The principal ingredient in this obscurity was symbolism. The apocalyptist said his piece not in syllogisms but in visual images which had to be translated before they conveyed their meaning to the reader. This applied not only to the composite symbol but even to its details (eyes stood for knowledge, wings for speed, legs for stability etc.), to its colours (white symbolized victory, red violence, scarlet majesty etc.), and to its numbers (four indicated the corners of the earth, seven perfection, a

---

* Designed as it was for times of persecution, most of the apocalyptic literature can be dated around the three great falls of Jerusalem in 170 B.C., 63 B.C. and A.D. 70.

thousand an immeasurable quantity etc.).* Indeed, once the
rules of the game were granted, an almost infinite series of
meaningful variations suggested themselves: if seven stood for
perfection, then eight stood for superperfection, six for the
failure to reach perfection, three and a half for the imperfection
which cannot last, and so on.† Superimposed, these symbols
might well be inconsistent with each other on the merely visual
level. But they were never meant to be a mere acrobatic
exercise for the imagination. The reader knew how to translate
them immediately into intellectual terms, that is into the ideas
of knowledge, victory, majesty, etc. for which they stood.

The symbols were largely borrowed in the first place from the
later prophets like Ezekiel, Zechariah and Joel who had begun
to abandon a direct method of preaching in favour of the
description of ecstasies and visions. In the course of the history
of apocalyptic writing other symbols were added to these, to
form part of the stock-in-trade of those who wished to express
themselves in this medium. To describe a vision it was no
longer necessary to experience a real ecstasy: the ingredients
were already available and needed only the hand of the artist to
arrange into a pattern. The imagery became conventional, and
was so universally recognized as 'apocalyptic idiom' that Christ
himself did not hesitate to use it to describe the Fall of Jerusalem which he promised would take place within a generation
of his speaking (Matt. 24$^{1-35}$).

---

* Our facility in the manipulation of numbers is a comparatively modern
achievement. The Egyptian hieroglyph for a thousand is a man holding his
hands up in despair, as much as to say: 'Who can count that far?'

† The fact that the moon's phases last seven days, and that there are
seven planets in the heavens, had long made seven a sacred number among
the ancients. Could they have been further influenced by the fact that it is
the sum of three (the 'divine' number) and four (the 'four corners of the
earth') and so represented for them the perfect action of God on the world?
If so it would explain why twelve (the product of these numbers) was also
a sacred number, and six (the half of twelve) as baneful as three and a half
(the half of seven).

John's Apocalypse

That outline of apocalyptic literature in general should throw
some light on the book we are discussing, which in its opening
words claims to be a piece of literature of the type that has been
described:

> The Apocalypse of Jesus Christ, given him by God to show to his
> servants.

Obviously there are points of difference; this book does
not claim to have been written centuries before its publication,
nor does the author hide behind the mask of anonymity: he
openly gives his name, John, and knows that it will be recognized by his readers. But the book does nevertheles claim
to be an 'apocalypse', and therefore presumably asks to be
interpreted according to the rules of that literary form. It
deliberately sets out to use the idiom common to this kind of
literature, and therefore presumably asks that this idiom be
recognized for what it is, and not taken literally. It will be
obscure, but intentionally so, like all other works of this sort,
and we must not be surprised if we experience difficulty in
finding our way round it. At the same time it will not be the
complete enigma which so many people imagine it to be, the
sealed book which will only make sense when the last trumpet
sounds and John will turn round to say: 'There, I told you so'.
As in other apocalypses, we must presume that the visions are
symbolic descriptions of actual events in history. Nor will these
historical events be in the vague and distant future which the
reader has not yet seen.* As in all other books of this kind, they
will be events in the present and the past. Even though they
are described in the future tense, the first readers of the book
will have already experienced them. Of course they only provide
the 'build-up', the necessary background without which God's

---

* It is interesting that this sort of interpretation, in which all the history of
Europe was read into the Apocalypse, did not begin until the Middle Ages·
It has been common enough ever since, with a different set of applications
for each succeeding century as the end of the world has failed to come.
Before the Middle Ages, the literary form of apocalypse was still understood.

final victory would be isolated and meaningless. This future victory does still lie outside the readers' experience, and it will be the author's aim to focus their attention on it. But it remains true that most of the events to which he will refer, six out of every seven in fact, will be events which he and his readers know have already taken place. This was simply the accepted way of writing apocalypses. Anyone who finds references to events centuries distant from the book's first readers may rest assured that he has misinterpreted the author. He is concerned for the most part with things which have already happened. And that is why we must know something of the historical circumstances in which he was writing.

Historical Background

All apocalypses were written in times of persecution and crisis. John's Apocalypse is no exception. It presumes as its background the Emperor-worship and Gnosticism of the second half of the first century, and the difficulties experienced by the young Christian churches of Asia Minor under the impact of these two forces.

Emperor-worship thrives on eastern soil. Grandiose titles like 'Son of God', 'Divine Manifestation' and 'Saviour' are as common in modern Japan as they were in ancient Mesopotamia. In themselves they indicate no more than that the easterner's court-style is more flamboyant than that of the sober westerner. The Greek emperors had readily accepted the titles as an expression of loyalty, and found them a convenient means of ensuring the unity of their sprawling dominions; and Romans like Augustus and Tiberius who inherited their empire interpreted them in much the same way, as titles of honour. Their government officials in the provinces, however, were not so willing to play down the meaning of the titles, especially in the East where the constant threat of Parthian invasion seemed to make it necessary to emphasize the divine right by which the emperor maintained the peace of the empire. And the more

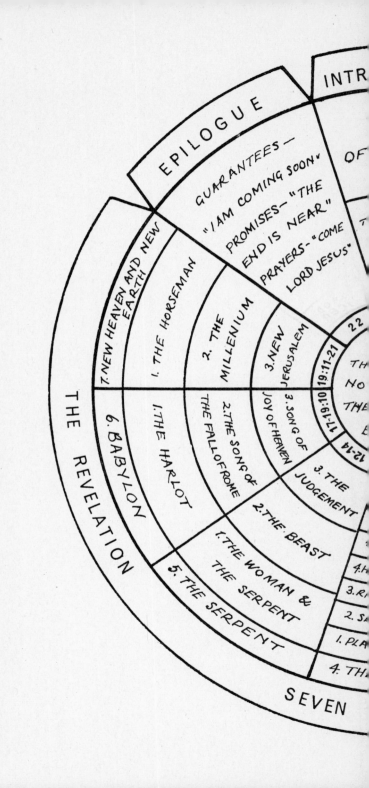

Covering Letter

TO THE 7 CHURCHES

1. EPHESIS
2. SMYRNA
3. PERGAMUM
4. THYATIRA
5. SARDIS
6. PHILA-DELPHIA
7. LAOD-ICEA

1. THE LAMB

1. THE THRONE

2. THE SCROLL

3. THE LAMB

2-3

CAN-
BUT
IS

4-5

6-7

8-11

7. SILENCE IN HEAVEN

6. COSMIC SIGNS

5. WHITE ROBED MARTYRS

4. PALE HORSE

3. BLACK HORSE

2. RED HORSE

1. WHITE HORSE

2. THE 7 SEALS

7. VOICES IN HEAVEN

6. ARMY OF HORSEMEN

5. OPENING OF HELL

4. ECLIPSE

3. FALLING STAR

2. MOUNTAIN OF FIRE

1. HAIL, FIRE, FLOOD

3. THE 7 TRUMPETS

- ERUPTION

ION
E
OK
LY
T
E
OOD
OD
RES
VLS

ESSIONS OF THE SAME THEME

extreme of the Roman emperors encouraged them in this interpretation. In the 60s of the first century Nero began to build temples and altars in his own name, to institute a priesthood dedicated to his worship, and to demand that sacrifice should be offered in his honour. In the 90s Domitian found that even this did not satisfy his vanity. He was prepared to liquidate even those of his family whom he did not regard as being sufficiently serious about the divine honours he demanded, and insisted that his imperial decrees should begin with the words *Dominus et Deus Noster*. To this even the unimpressionable Romans objected. The Christians, who acknowledged only one Lord and one God, were bound to object more strongly still. In the 50s and 60s their leaders had been anxious to insist on loyalty to the government, so that no colour should be given to the charge that their beliefs were disruptive of good order (see for instance Matt. 22^{21}, Rom. 13^{1-7}, 1 Tim. 2^2, Tit. 3^1, 1 Pet. 2^{13-17}). In the 80s and 90s we find them far less ready to declare such unqualified loyalty, and even demanding that at a certain point the Christian must register his protest, even if it meant ostracism, persecution, and eventually martyrdom.

That this protest constituted a danger for the Church was obvious. The danger inherent in first century *Gnosticism* was less obvious, and therefore more insidious. By the second and third centuries, this heresy had become sufficiently distinct from orthodox Christianity for the Church Fathers (Justin, Irenaeus, Tertullian, Hippolytus) to mount a concerted attack against it. But in its earlier and more fluid form, it was sufficiently imprecise to pass for an interpretation of Christianity which could deceive even the elect. St Paul had to fight against it in Corinth and Colossae, and St Jude and the writer of 2 Peter in other parts of Asia Minor, while St John's excited reaction to it in his epistles reveals what a strong foothold it had gained in Ephesus.

Gnosticism was an attempt to explain Christianity along the lines of the mystery-religions which flourished in the Middle East at the turn of the millenium. It was based on a perfectly orthodox desire to emphasize the utter transcendency of God, and to place an infinite distance between him and all that is worldly, earthly and human. It erred in concluding that even God himself could not bridge that infinite gap. For the divine to become available to mankind, it had to be gradually diluted by an infinite series of intermediaries. These demiurges or angelic beings, neither divine nor human, are the only means by which earthbound man can establish contact with the transcendent God.

Of these demiurges, Christ was merely the highest. Neither truly God nor truly man, he came as an intermediary to bring us the *gnosis* or knowledge of an otherwise unknowable God. The soul, that divine spark in each of us which the original Fall has imprisoned in an earthly body, is united to God by this knowledge, and so liberated from its prison house. The body itself remains unsaveable, as does the bulk of humanity, the common herd which continues to think of its body rather than its soul. Salvation is for the élite only, the gnostics who are in the *gnosis*.

The danger of this doctrine lay not simply in the manichean asceticism which it often implied (an attempt to assist the soul's liberation from the body), nor even in the utter immorality with which, by a kind of mad logic, it was often coupled (to sin with one's body was not to sin with the true self). It lay at the doctrinal level, in its emptying out of what was distinctive about Christianity. For the true Christian message was that God had not written off the human situation as hopeless, but had entered into the very heart of it to raise it, body and soul, to the divine level. In Christ, God had made himself one with men, had identified himself with the desperate condition of the lowest among them. He had not come like an aloof visitor from outer space to reveal to them an esoteric knowledge of another world; he had come as one of themselves, so that through his death and resurrection he could put into their hands the very life of heaven. To present his teaching as a mere piece of advanced thought for the intelligentsia was to deny the very meaning of the Good News, that in Christ God had become flesh.

Yet the fact was that a Gnostic interpretation of Christianity was gaining more and more adherents, especially in the philosophy-conscious Greek world.* The uncompromising stand taken by the New Testament writers on Christ's divinity, and their stubborn refusal to come to terms with Emperor-worship, was ridiculed as a piece of crude intolerance, a narrow-minded rejection of modern thought. The Christian communities of Asia Minor, recruited as they were mainly from the poorer classes, were ill-prepared for this intellectual onslaught. When the principles they were asked to hold firm brought them daily persecution as well, they may well have wondered if resistance was worth while. If Christ's triumph over death was the irreversible victory preached by the apostles, why was there not more evidence of it? They had constantly promised that he would return in glory to complete the work he had so manifestly left unfinished. Where were the signs that this was not any empty promise? Given the irrefutable facts of history, was it not inevitable that Christianity should either be slowly diluted into an innocuous eastern mystery-religion, or else be obliterated by Rome? Could the defenceless Church ever hold its own in this situation, let alone overcome and convert the mighty forces which were unleashing against it such hatred and violence?

The Apocalypse was written to assure the Church that it would. Over and over again it describes, in symbols with which the Church of the first century had already become familiar, the events of recent and present history. Each time the reader is to be reassured that this has been no haphazard series of events, but the ordered plan of a God who remains in supreme control of all history. Each time his eye is being focused on the inevitable conclusion to each series: God's final victory over the forces of evil.

* A danger which is always present in the Church among those for whom the only lapses are intellectual ones. This is not to say that there is not the equally great danger that some Christians will be blind to all lapses except moral ones.

The book's message, then, is clear: with the certainty of victory within his grasp, the reader is to stand firm. Were the situation to become even blacker than it already was, it would still be madness to give in. Who throws in the sponge in the last round? This message is expressed in terms designed to be meaningful to the Church of the first century; without some knowledge of the historical background many of its topical references will escape us. But its central theme is timeless, and not tied down to any particular historical period. The Church will always be under fire from a paganized world, if not here then elsewhere, if not today then tomorrow. Nor is this struggle a merely external one; the forces of evil will always infiltrate into the life of the Church itself, like the tares among the wheat, to hide from others—and even from itself—the reality it is striving to become. The message of the Apocalypse will therefore always be relevant, will always need to be repeated. Its details may have lost their meaning for many of its readers, but its central theme will make it for all time the triumphal song of the suffering and persecuted Church.

The Author

Who wrote this remarkable book? He calls himself the brother of his readers, a partner in their present sufferings (1^9). The tone in which he addresses them suggests that he holds a position of some authority over them (ch. 2-3), and indeed is on familiar terms with them—his name is sufficient to identify him. He gives his name four times: it is John ($1^{1,\ 4,\ 9}$, 22^8). The question remains, which John are we dealing with, the Apostle or someone else?

There is no easy answer to this question, since the arguments so far brought forward on both sides are equally cogent and almost equally venerable. In favour of the book's apostolic origin is the impressive list of second century Fathers—Justin, Irenaeus, Clement of Alexandria, Tertullian, Hippolytus—who accepted it without hesitation as the work of John the apostle.

The doubts which were raised later seem to have been due largely to the embarrassment caused when the third century Montanist revivalists became the principal patrons of the Utopia apparently promised in ch. 20, and a need was felt to find someone other than an apostle on whom to father this strange doctrine.* Apart from this misunderstanding it would seem that no one would have questioned the book's authorship, which the West continued to accept unanimously even after the third century contretemps. After all, it was argued, were not the themes of which it treated—Lamb and Shepherd, Water and Manna, Judgment and Temple—specifically the ones St John's Gospel dealt with? Certainly the contrasts it constantly uses— the Lamb versus the Beast, the Bride versus the Harlot, Jerusalem versus Babylon, etc.—are entirely Johannine in inspiration, even though the Gospel and epistles use different examples to make the same point. And so too is the circular and recapitulatory style which makes each chapter simply a repetition—not a continuation—of those that precede it (see below). Finally, there is the intricate use of the number seven, which has always been recognized as forming the framework of the Apocalypse, but which it is now realized has influenced the structure of the Gospel too.† These arguments, among others,‡

---

* An otherwise unknown 'John the presbyter' was the favourite candidate. The suggestion has allowed his shadowy figure to bedevil Johannine criticism ever since, particularly in reference to the two epistles which St John signed under the title of 'The presbyter'. It has been drily observed that when John the presbyter has retired into the obscurity from which he should never have emerged, scholars may be able to credit him with the existence which he no doubt deserves. On the utopian millenium, see below pp. 117–121.

† The Gospel recounts seven miracles, appeals to seven witnesses to Christ, divides the public ministry into seven weeks, recounts seven of Christ's sayings beginning with the pregnant words 'I am', etc.

‡ For instance the fact that the Apocalypse is the only New Testament writing outside the Gospel and epistles of St John which calls Christ the Word of God (Apoc. 19^{13}, see the opening lines of the Gospel and (?) of the First Epistle), and finds a reference to the crucifixion in the strange oracle of Zech. 12^9-13^1 (Apoc. 1^7, see John 3^{14-15}, 7^{38}, 19^{34-37}). In fact, when this prophetical text is explicitly quoted, both Apoc. 1^7 and John 19^{37} agree to use a Greek text different from that of the Septuagint.

have sufficient weight to convince many scholars that no one else but the apostle John could have written the Apocalypse.

There are others, however, who maintain just as strongly that the Apocalypse is the one book which could not have been written by the author of the Fourth Gospel. And they appeal not simply to internal arguments of style and vocabulary, but to a tradition whose age has made it almost as respectable as the other. It was Denis, the third century bishop of Alexandria, who first questioned the apostolic origin of the book, saying that he could not find in it one syllable which could have been written by St John, who in any case would not name himself 'John' as the author of this book does, but style himself as elsewhere 'The disciple whom Jesus loved' or 'The elder'. He was so firm in his view that he persuaded giants like Eusebius of Caesarea, Cyril of Jerusalem, Gregory Nazianzen, John Chrysostom and Theodoretus to agree with him. The East in fact found it extremely difficult to accept the Apocalypse as the work of an apostle (the Syriac versions resolutely refused to find room for it among the books of the New Testament), and modern scholars have not been slow to add fuel to these doubts. It has been pointed out that although the Greek of the Gospel and epistles is not of a high literary standard it is at least felicitous and grammatical, whereas the Apocalypse uses a strange and barbarous language with tenses, declensions, conjugations and vocabulary not found anywhere else in the Greek world.* In fact the same literary analysis which proves that the Gospel and the First Epistle are from the same hand proves that the

---

* Even Fr Martindale, who stoutly defends the Johannine authorship of the book, has to admit that 'in every superficial way, the apocalyptic diction, with its amazing mistakes in sheer Greek grammar and syntax, its violent dislocations, its foreign use of words and constructions, is seemingly as unlike as can be to that of the Fourth Gospel' (*St John and the Apocalypse*, Sheed & Ward, 1958, p. viii-ix). The outlandishness of the Greek is inevitably lost in translation, which cannot afford to render 1^4, for instance, as an utterly faithful translation would have to render: 'Grace to you and peace from the He Is and the He Was and the He Will Come.' The language has been compared to the 'refugese' spoken by those who have emigrated too late in their lives to master the language of their new country.

Apocalypse is from a different hand. It is only possible to maintain that the same author wrote all three by appealing, as Martindale does,* to the disturbed state of one who had received such visions, and the hardship of the Patmos quarries where there was neither the leisure nor the opportunity for disciples to give the Apocalypse the same literary polish they had given to the Gospel. But there is no evidence that the Greek of the Gospel is not St John's own,† or that the visions of the Apocalypse were not composed in as cold a blood as those of any other apocalyptic literature.

Perhaps it is the theology of the book which weighs most heavily with those who are reluctant to ascribe it to St John. If it includes many themes which may be called Johannine, it omits many more which one may have had a right to expect from a writing of St John. Life and death, light and darkness, truth and falsehood, Father and Son, faith and love, Christ's flesh and blood, the indwelling of Christ's Spirit, the Christian's adoptive sonship—these are what might be called St John's most characteristic concepts. Yet none of them appears in the Apocalypse in those characteristic terms. The book even uses different terms for those ideas it *does* have in common with the Gospel.‡ Would St John have done such a thing? Is it like St John, one of the most original of writers, to borrow as heavily as this author does from the Old Testament,§ and indeed from St Paul?‖

* *Op. cit.*, p. ix-x.

† There are plenty of indications that the *structure* of the Fourth Gospel is due to the editorial work of St John's disciples, but nothing to suggest that they were in any way responsible for its *language*.

‡ E.g. *arnion* for St John's *amnos* (lamb), and 'inhabitants of the earth' for St John's 'world'.

§ Within the 404 verses of the Apocalypse, 518 Old Testament quotations have been counted, some of them knitted together so tightly that it needs an expert to unravel them. Apoc. 15[3-4], for instance, is a mosaic of quotations from Exod. 15[2], Pss. 98[2], 110[2], 139[14], 1 Chron. 16[9], Zech. 14[9], Jerem. 10[7], Exod. 9[16] and Micah 7[15]. There is no reason why St John should not have done this as easily as anyone else. But he does not do so in his other writings.

‖ In the very first chapter, v. 5 is a direct quotation of Col. 1[18], v. 6 of Rom. 16[27], and v. 7 of 2 Cor. 1[20].

These arguments, among others,* have forced many scholars
—Catholic ones included—to the conclusion that the Apocalypse was the work not of John the apostle but of a disciple who
had imbibed much of his master's theology and style. This
disciple may himself have been called John,† or may simply
have assumed the name of his master, in the style of other
apocalypses, to indicate that the message his book was putting
across was not his own but St John's. In either case the book
would have continued to be linked with the name of St John in
much the same way as the Epistle to the Hebrews was always
linked with the name of St Paul, even though both were
recognized as not stemming from the apostles as directly as
their other writings.

To sum up, the arguments in favour of St John as the author
of this book are met at every point by equally strong arguments
against him. Since there is nothing to force us to come to any
conclusion on the matter, the question may perhaps best be left
open, in the knowledge that it would be unwise to be too
dogmatic on either side.

The Structure and Date of the Book

On the subject of the book's structure it would be even less wise
to be over-dogmatic, especially since it is closely connected with
the widely disputed date of its composition. Not that the

* For instance the fact that the author of the Apocalypse, though he
claims to be a prophet, seems to distinguish himself from the apostles, to
whom he looks back nostalgically, rather as the author of 2 Peter 3^2 does, as
belonging to a past age (18^{20}). Certainly it would be difficult to conceive of
an apostle speaking of himself as a foundation stone of the New Jerusalem
(21^{14}). Some scholars would add, as the clinching argument, the violent
contrast between the eschatology of this book, which constantly points to the
future for the final fulfilment of God's plans, and that of St John, who sees
those plans fully realized in the present. But unless one is to regard them
all as inauthentic, there are several texts in St John's Gospel which
look forward to a fullness of salvation which can only be realized in the
future (see John $5^{28-29, \ 45}$, 6^{39-44}, 12^{48}, 21^{22}); and the Apocalypse itself, as
will be seen later, has much in common with St John's 'realized eschatology'.

† John Mark, the author of the Second Gospel, has been suggested; or a
John mentioned by Eusebius as having been ordained bishop of Ephesus by
the Apostle at the end of the first century.

general shape of the book is under question: it needs no very critical eye to see that it is made up of a central section sandwiched between a prologue (ch. 1-3) and an epilogue (22^{6-21}). But how is one to understand the make-up of the central section, where revelation is piled upon revelation and vision follows new vision? Where does one vision end and the next begin? What is the connection between them? Is the whole thing meant to stop every now and again and then start again from the beginning, or is it all intended to be one long sequence?

A closer examination of the text, far from answering these questions, only adds more. One frequently gets the impression that the order of the book could be improved by transposing one or other of the visions, or one or other of the chapters. Sometimes a few verses seem suddenly to disturb the context and one feels that the whole presentation would be so much clearer if they could be omitted. More strangely still, it will happen that some person or thing will be presented to the reader as if for the first time ('a lamb') when in fact he has already come across it in a previous chapter and was expecting to read '*the* lamb'. Or it will happen the other way round, that reference is made to '*the* altar' when the reader has not even been introduced to it yet. Just as disturbing are the inconsistencies, which render it difficult or impossible to make the references of one chapter fit another.* In view of this confusion, it is not surprising to learn that there has always been violent disagreement about the date of the book's composition, with some finding in it unmistakeable references to Nero's persecution in the 60s of the first century, and others just as unmistakeable references to that of Domitian in the 90s. The disagreement has been there from the time the book was first critically studied in the second century, and is not resolved yet; eminent scholars can still be quoted for either view.

* For example, the 'Beast' of ch. 13 is clearly meant to be identified with the Roman emperor Nero, who lived at a time when the Jerusalem Temple was still standing (11^1, 14^{15}). Yet in ch. 17 the same Beast is just as clearly someone other than Nero who is stated to be dead, and 12^{17-18} presumes Jerusalem to have been destroyed and its Christians dispersed.

How is one to account for these facts? Is it that the book is basically a Jewish composition of the 60s,* adapted and given a Christian prologue and epilogue during the persecution of the 90s? Or is it simply that the author writing in the 90s has made use of notes which he had made earlier in the 60s? Or has he used several pre-existing apocalypses of different dates, and either haphazardly interwoven them or clumsily joined them end to end? All these hypotheses have their champions. The International Critical Commentary (R. H. Charles, 1920 and 1950) proposes an even more drastic solution by making a hypothetical editor responsible for all the book's difficulties; but then it would make a farce of Scripture studies to write off as the interpolation of an imbecile anything which is inconsistent with one's own interpretation.† The Jerusalem Bible (M. E. Boismard O.P., 1950 and 1956) has made a more careful investigation of the book's many 'doublets', and has concluded that the present text is a fusion of two different drafts of the same apocalypse, drawn up by a disciple of St John at two different dates, one under Nero and the other under Domitian.

---

* The very first vision in ch. 4 goes for half its length without any reference to Christ. The 'sevens' of ch. 6-11 and 15-16 (see below) would need very little editing to turn them into purely pre-Christian apocalyptic visions.

† Under Charles' pungent pen this imaginary editor takes on considerable solidity: 'Unhappily the prophet (John) did not live to revise his work... This task fell, to the misfortune of all students of the Apocalypse, into the hands of a very unintelligent disciple ... profoundly ignorant of his master's thought. If he had left his master's thought as he found it, its teaching would not have been the unintelligible mystery it has been to subsequent ages; but unhappily he intervened repeatedly, rearranging the text in some cases, adding to it in others . . .' On the anathema of 22^{18-19} Charles writes: '(This) interpolation exhibits the editor at his worst. Having taken the most unwarrantable liberties with his author's text by perverting its teaching in some passages and by his interpolations making it wholly unintelligible in others, he sets the crown on his misdemeanours by invoking an anathema on any person who should in any respect follow the method which had the sanction of his own example. By this and other like unwarrantable devices this shallow-brained fanatic and celibate (!), whose dogmatism varies directly with the narrowness of his understanding, has often stood between John and his readers for nearly 2000 years. But such obscurantism cannot outlive the limits assigned to it; the reverent and patient research of the present age (! !) is steadily discovering and bringing to light the teaching of this great Christian prophet . . .'

The reader must be left to judge the merits of this hypothesis from the detailed analysis made elsewhere,* but the dismemberment of the text it involves seems excessive.† Would it not be possible to dissever a symphony, for example, in much the same sort of way, and find in its interplaying themes traces of two different compositions? Does not this hypothesis, like the others, look for far more sequence than can be expected from a Johannine writing?

The Gospel and epistles of St John stand out from the rest of the New Testament writings for their concentric or circular structure. There is not, as in the other Gospels and epistles, any progress made from one theme to the next, because St John has only one theme, which he presents in all its fullness on the very first page, only to continue reconsidering it again and again from new viewpoints. Is it not likely that the same plan has been followed in the Apocalypse, which, if it is not directly from the hand of St John, certainly stems from his school of thought? If difficulties of sequence and consistence are felt by those who try to find a forward movement in the book, is it not probable that there *is* no forward movement, and that the Apocalypse simply says the same thing over and over again in statements which are deliberately parallel with each other, and therefore reaches its climax not at the end of the last chapter but at the end of each section?

This 'theory of recapitulation', as it is known, is not new. It was recognized as early as the fourth century by the very first man to write a commentary on this difficult book, Victorinus of Pettau. It does not solve all the book's problems, but it does suggest a fairly simple plan for the book as we now have it, which seems to have been put together in the 90s of the first century:

A. Prologue: ch. 1-3
   (a preface, an inaugural vision and a covering letter)

* See the *Revue Biblique* 56 (1949), p. 507-541, and 59(1952), p. 161-181.
† For example, in ch. 18, verses 1-3, 9-13, 15-19, 21 and 24 have to represent 'text I', and verses 4-8, 14, 20, 22 and 23 'text II'.

B. The Revelation: ch. 4-21
   (Christ's triumph revealed in 7 parallel statements)
   1. The lamb ch. 4-5
   2. The seven seals ch. 6-7
   3. The seven trumpets ch. 8-11
   4. The serpent ch. 12-14
   5. The seven bowls of wrath ch. 15-16
   6. Babylon ch. 17^1-19^{10}
   7. The defeat of evil ch. 19^{11}-22^5
C. Epilogue ch. 22

It is upon this plan that the commentary which follows is based.

II THE PROLOGUE

Chapters 1 to 3

The prologue to the Apocalypse covers the first three chapters, and is made up of a title, a greeting, an inaugural vision and a covering letter addressed to the seven churches for whom the book is destined.

The Title

The first three verses of the prologue form a kind of title for the whole book, stating the contents and the scope of what is to follow.

> **1** ¹The revelation of Jesus Christ, which God gave him to show to his servants what must soon take place; and he made it known by sending his angel to his servant John, ²who bore witness to the word of God and to the testimony of Jesus Christ, even to all that he saw. ³Blessed is he who reads aloud the words of the prophecy, and blessed are those who hear, and who keep what is written therein; for the time is near.

What John wishes to present is an *apokalypsis*, that is to say an 'unveiling' of something so far hidden from the reader. We have already seen that the word was used as a literary device, and need not involve the revelation of anything that the readers of the book do not already know. But this does not mean that they are wasting their time in reading the book. For the readers John has in mind, pressed hard on all sides by a hostile world, it is

possible to be blind to things before their very eyes. It is not
events that are revealed to the readers of an apocalypse—they
are living in the midst of them—but their meaning, their
purpose, their design, their function. They must be given an
assurance that the trials they are undergoing are part of the plan
of God, who has them all in his control and who out of them will
fashion the salvation of his people. That is why John's book,
like all apocalypses, concerns 'what must soon take place', 'for
the time (of fulfilment) is near.' To find in John's words
references to persons and things centuries distant from his first
readers is obviously to misunderstand what he had to say.

The angel of v. 1 is part of the literary form of apocalypse;
the whole supposition is that we are dealing with heavenly
secrets to which only the angels are privy and which only they
can make known. All apocalyptic literature abounds in angels·
But the angel is only an intermediary. The source of the
revelation which John has to impart to us is Jesus Christ, who
is in his own person the complete self-revelation of God, the
Word which God has uttered in order to tell us all that there is
to be known of himself. It is for this reason that John concludes
with a blessing upon those who hear the Apocalypse read aloud,
for it was meant to take its place in the public proclamation of
God's Word in the Church's liturgy.

Three things are worth remarking upon in these opening
verses of the book: their breathless style,* the reference to
Christ as the Word of God (implicitly in v. 1, if not explicitly
in v. 2), and the anxiety that the reader should pay attention to
what he is reading. All three touches might be called typical of
St John: both his Gospel and his first epistle start in exactly the
same breathless way† with a presentation of Christ as the

---

* This is not so noticeable in the smooth English of the RSV used here,
but a literal rendering would read something like this: 'The Revelation of
Jesus Christ, which God gave him to show to his servants, what must soon
take place, and he showed (it), having sent (it) by his Angel, to his servant
John, who bore witness to the Word of God, and the witness (is) of Jesus
Christ, all that he saw.'

† The epistle goes through 86 words before it arrives at the first full stop.

culminating point of God's revelation* and an appeal to be taken seriously.† As has already been shown, this does not necessarily prove anything about the authorship of the Apocalypse, but it does indicate the school of thought from which it originates.

The Greeting

Since this book is designed to be sent out as a letter, it begins with a greeting to its addressees, and in the style of other New Testament letters includes in the greeting a summary of all that is to follow.

> **1** ⁴John to the seven churches that are in Asia:
> Grace to you and peace from him who is and who was and is to come, and from the seven spirits who are before his throne, ⁵and from Jesus Christ the faithful witness, the firstborn of the dead, and the ruler of kings on earth.
> To him who loves us and has freed us from our sins by his blood ⁶and made us a kingdom, priests to his God and Father, to him be glory and dominion for ever and ever. Amen.
> ⁷Behold, he is coming with the clouds, and every eye will see him, every one who pierced him; and all tribes of the earth will wail on account of him. Even so. Amen.
> ⁸'I am the Alpha and the Omega,' says the Lord God, who is and who was and who is to come, the Almighty.

The book is addressed to the 'seven churches in Asia'. These will later be specifically named, and a glance at a map will show that they stand on a circular route running inland from Ephesus and back over a distance of some 300 miles. A similar circuit in England would run from London to Brighton, Southampton, Newbury, Oxford, Buckingham, Bedford and back to London. They would have been chosen deliberately as centres for communicating the book's message further. But the choice of seven, not six or eight, is also deliberate; in apocalyptic language

---

* See John 1¹ and 1 John 1².

† 'We have *seen* his glory' John 1¹⁴; 'That which . . . we have *heard*, which we have *seen* with our own eyes, which we have *looked upon* and *touched* with our own hands . . .' 1 John 1¹.

this number stands for totality,* and it is to all the churches of
Asia, indeed to all the churches of Christendom, that the
message of this book is addressed.

The greeting offered to them is one with which most of the
New Testament epistles open, a combination of the 'grace' by
which the Greeks wished each other goodwill, and the 'peace'
with which the Hebrews have always saluted each other.
Christians, of course, had already charged these words with a
new meaning: the goodwill they wished each other was God's
and the peace for which they longed was the restoration of
harmony between God and men. It is interesting that the
Roman emperors regarded themselves as the source of grace,
favour and peace (the *Pax Romana*). For the Christian, these
blessings could only come from the Triune God, that is to say
from the eternal Being who is described almost untranslatably
as the 'He is, He was, He will come',† from the sevenfold
Spirit proceeding from him, and from Jesus Christ.‡

Once arrived at the name of Jesus Christ, the author develops
his titles. For the Christ he wishes to present to his readers,
tempted to despair over the events they are living through, is
despite all appearances to the contrary the Lord, the master, the
ruler of all things. The title was one which the Caesars loved to
give to themselves, but it belongs by right to the man Jesus
Christ alone, who in his resurrection had overcome the forces
which separate mankind from God and been raised to the right
hand of the Father in heaven. Nor had he made this transition
merely for his own benefit. The resurrection had made him the
'firstborn of the dead', the first of the many of his brethren who

* See above pp. 13–14.

† The atrocious Greek of this title, repeated in v. 8, can only be explained as an attempt to convey the meaning of the divine name Yahweh
(literally 'He is') as Jewish theologians had developed it by the Christian
era: the Eternal One, unbounded by time, who ever was and ever will be.

‡ There can be little doubt that the greeting is a trinitarian one; for
anyone as nervous about Gnostic angel-worship as the author of this book,
it would be unthinkable to link seven spirit 'angels' so immediately with the
Father and the Son. He places the Holy Spirit second in his list so that he
may conclude on Jesus Christ, the theme of his whole book.

were to share his victory, and so the witness to God's fidelity, the living guarantee that God is faithful to his promise to save his people. The resurrection, as John will point out again and again, is the key to the whole of God's plan of salvation.

The two prayers which are added to this enthusiastic description of Christ are probably pieces in actual use in the liturgy of the day: the *Amen* at the end of each would suggest this. The glory and power which the Roman emperors have claimed for themselves belong to him alone, because he alone has loved us* to the extent of delivering us from our slavery to sin and making us, like the Israel of old, a kingdom of priests, a people utterly taken up with the worship of God. This is the Christ who is to come again like Daniel's Son of Man† to pass judgment for good or evil on all men, and like the mysterious pierced figure of Zechariah 12¹⁰ to arouse for evil or good their remorse for their sin. The prayers conclude with the signature of God himself, the Beginning and End of all things, whose eternity‡ is the ultimate guarantee that the last word will be his.

These few verses of greeting are perhaps typical of the Apocalypse's style. The margin of a good critical text will indicate how many Old Testament texts have been quoted and alluded to. But the author has summarized the New Testament too, with his reference to the Trinity, the incarnation, the crucifixion, the resurrection, the redemption, the second coming and the world's judgment. And he has expressed these ideas in such a way as to present the theme of the whole book. The rest of the book will simply repeat what he has already in miniature expressed here.

---

* It is interesting that these are two of the ideas uppermost in the mind of St John when he is describing the act by which Christ redeemed us. See John 15¹³, 1 John 3¹⁶, John 19³⁷, 1 John 5⁶.

† See below on 1¹³.

‡ Alpha is first letter of the Greek alphabet and Omega the last. The rabbis had used their own Hebrew alphabet in the same way to call God the aleph (first letter), mem (middle letter) and tau (last letter). The word formed by these three letters means 'reliability', and comes from the same root as our familiar *Amen*.

The Inaugural Vision

The books of Isaiah, Jeremiah and Ezekiel each begin with a description of the vision with which the prophets were given their commission. John here does the same. His inaugural vision, an overwhelming one, came to him 'in the Spirit'* while he was serving his time on the island of Patmos, one of Rome's penal settlements off the coast of Asia Minor.

1 9I, John, your brother, who share with you in Jesus the tribulation and the kingdom and the patient endurance, was on the island called Patmos on account of the word of God and the testimony of Jesus. 10I was in the Spirit on the Lord's day, and I heard behind me a loud voice like a trumpet 11saying, 'Write what you see in a book and send it to the seven churches, to Ephesus and to Smyrna and to Pergamum and to Thyatira and to Sardis and to Philadelphia and to Laodicea.'

12Then I turned to see the voice that was speaking to me, and on turning I saw seven golden lampstands, 13and in the midst of the lampstands one like a Son of Man, clothed with a long robe and with a golden girdle round his breast; 14his head and his hair were white as white wool, white as snow; his eyes were like a flame of fire, 15his feet were like burnished bronze, refined as in a furnace, and his voice was like the sound of many waters; 16in his right hand he held seven stars, from his mouth issued a sharp two-edged sword, and his face was like the sun shining in full strength.

17When I saw him, I fell at his feet as though dead. But he laid his right hand upon me, saying, 'Fear not, I am the first and the last, 18and the living one; I died, and behold I am alive for evermore, and I have the keys of Death and Hades. 19Now write what you see, what is and what is to take place hereafter. 20As for the mystery of the seven stars which you saw in my right hand, and the seven golden lampstands, the seven stars are the angels of the seven churches and the seven lampstands are the seven churches.'

'Son of Man' is a title frequently given to Christ in the Gospels. It is usually taken to refer to the weak and fragile humanity with which Christ had identified himself in becoming man. It would be foolish to deny the importance of this aspect

---

* The fact that a great number of apocalypses use this literary device to introduce their message leaves the reality or unreality of John's ecstasy an open question.

of the title, but it is not the aspect which the Gospels most emphasize. They make it clear that the basic reference behind the title is to the mysterious otherworldly figure, scarcely distinct from God himself, first mentioned in the earliest of the apocalypses, the book of Daniel (7^{13}), as coming in glory to bring heaven to earth. Certainly it is in this sense that the figure is taken up in the other apocalyptic books of the last century B.C., which had abandoned all hope of a political restoration of Israel's kingdom, and looked instead for the utterly spiritual kingdom brought from heaven by God himself. Certainly it is this sense which Christ himself had in mind when he used the title of himself. He wished to avoid the nationalistic overtones inherent in the current titles of the Messiah, 'Son of David' or 'Son of God', and to insist that he was the far more heavenly 'Son of Man'.

The Apocalypse, even more than the Gospels, underlines this divine aspect of Christ. It does not even hesitate to take up both the figures in Daniel's vision—the heavenly Son of Man and the eternal Ancient of Days*—and describe Christ in terms of both. So easily does John attribute divinity to Christ. In fact, apart from the long robe (a reference to Christ's priesthood, see Exod. 28^4) and the golden girdle (a reference to his kingship, see 1 Macc. 11^{58}), all the ensuing details are taken from Old Testament descriptions of God and his piercing wisdom (the fiery eyes, see Ps. 7^{10}, Jerem. 17^{10}), his unmoveability (the brass feet, see Ezek. 1^{27}, Dan. 2), his irresistible power (the rushing waters, see Ezek. 4^{32}), his supreme command of all things (the seven stars, see Job 38^{31}), his readiness to punish sinners (the two-edged sword, see Isa. 34^6 and compare Hebr. 4^{12}), his unapproachable majesty (the sun-like face, see Isa. 60^{19} and compare Matt. 17^2), his eternity (the first and last, see Isa. 44^6, 48^{12}), and his sovereignty over life and death (the keys of Hades, see Deut. 32^{29}, Tobit 13^1). Before such an awesome figure

---

* The detail of the snow-white hair is taken from Dan. 7^9 in reference to God himself. It is a symbol of his eternity.

John falls on his face in sheer terror,* only to be told that the vision is to give him confidence. These divine prerogatives truly belong to the Christ who overcame death and so entered into the world of God. His resurrection is the guarantee that the forces of evil are conquered and that the victory is already won.

Such is the Christ who walks among the seven lampstands which are echoed by the seven stars in his hand. John explains that the lampstands symbolize the churches to whom the Apocalypse is addressed, and that the stars are their angels, linking them with the Christ who is compared to the sun. The explanation of the 'angels' as the bishops of these churches, common in the West, is based on the fact that they are later reprimanded for the shortcomings of their charges. But this interpretation has read too much of our sophisticated angelology back into the Apocalypse, which uses the same word throughout for what are undoubtedly meant to *be* angels. The East has never hesitated to interpret them quite literally as the guardian angels of the churches in their care. This follows the Jewish concept of a world utterly ruled by angels, who fight against each other for their protégés,† and can therefore be held responsible and rebuked for their faults.

But for the moment the author's emphasis is on the confidence that this picture is meant to inspire. Christ is in the midst of his churches, and holds even their angels in his right hand. They have no reason for fear. The vision again summarizes the whole book, and the joyful assurance that its readers must have in the protecting presence of the Christ who 'died but behold is alive for evermore'.

The Seven Churches

The prologue concludes with a covering letter addressed to seven individual Christian communities in Asia Minor. It has

---

* The reader is meant to be reminded of the many places in the Old Testament which inform us that the one whom no sinful man can see and remain alive is God. See for instance Exod. 19[21], 33[20], Levit. 16[2], Judges 13[22], Isa. 6[5].

† See especially Dan. 10[13, 20, 21].

already been mentioned above that these seven are a symbol of totality, and stand for the whole Church in Asia, and eventually for all Christian communities anywhere in the world: all of them will in their own time and in their own way stand in need of the reproof, the correction, the consolation and the encouragement offered here. Nevertheless, the seven have not been chosen at random. The many discreet topical references John makes to their geographical, political and cultural situation indicates that he knew these churches intimately; and although he addresses them all in a fairly stereotyped manner—a title of Christ, a word of praise and/or blame, a reproach and/or a promise—the words are chosen with the utmost care to strike home to their readers.

1. Ephesus

2 ¹To the angel of the church in Ephesus write: 'The words of him who holds the seven stars in his right hand, who walks among the seven golden lampstands.

²'I know your works, your toil and your patient endurance, and how you cannot bear evil men but have tested those who call themselves apostles but are not, and found them to be false; ³I know you are enduring patiently and bearing up for my name's sake, and you have not grown weary. ⁴But I have this against you, that you have abandoned the love you had at first. ⁵Remember then from what you have fallen, repent and do the works you did at first. If not, I will come to you and remove your lampstand from its place, unless you repent. ⁶Yet this you have, you hate the works of the Nicolaitans, which I also hate. ⁷He who has an ear, let him hear what the Spirit says to the churches. To him who conquers I will grant to eat of the tree of life, which is in the paradise of God.'

The principal seaport on the coast, Ephesus was in New Testament times a natural gateway between East and West, and the capital of the Roman province of Asia. Its church also naturally took precedence over the other churches in the province, and is here fittingly addressed by the Christ 'who holds the seven stars in his right hand, who walks among the seven golden lampstands,' that is to say, by the Christ who rules the Christian communities ruled by Ephesus. Its Christians are praised for their endurance under persecution, and for their constancy in rejecting the preaching of unauthorized Christian missionaries who were propounding a typically Gnostic compromise with paganism.* But together with the praise goes what might be called a characteristically Johannine reprimand: they have lost the love which had marked the early days of their Christianity, the charity without which the name of Christian is an empty title.† They are urged to reform themselves in this matter; otherwise they will be displaced as the religious leaders of Asia. John no doubt has in mind the fact that throughout its history Ephesus had suffered repeated displacement as its harbour silted up. There is probably also a topical reference to the famous sacred tree of the Ephesian Diana in the promise made to those who persevere: 'To him who conquers, I will grant to eat (not of that tree but of the infinitely more nourishing) tree of life which is in the paradise of God.'

2. Smyrna

2 ⁸And to the angel of the church in Smyrna write: 'The words of the first and the last, who died and came to life.

⁹"I know your tribulation and your poverty (but you are rich) and the slander of those who say that they are Jews and are not, but are a synagogue of Satan. ¹⁰Do not fear what you are about to suffer. Behold, the devil is about to throw some of you into prison, that you may be tested, and for ten days you will have tribulation. Be faithful unto death, and I will give you the crown of life. ¹¹He who has an ear, let him hear what the Spirit says to the churches. He who conquers shall not be hurt by the second death.'

---

* The name 'Nicolaitans' which is applied to them in v. 6 will be discussed later in reference to v. 15. It is interesting that St Paul had faced exactly the same kind of Gnostic interpretation of Christianity in these Asian towns (see Col. 2⁸⁻²³ and Eph. 5²⁻²⁰), and earlier had called those who tried to preach it in Corinth 'pseudo-apostles' (see 2 Cor. 11¹³).

† Both the Gospel and the epistles of St John emphasize this. What kind of Christian love the Ephesians were able to command in the first flush of their conversion is illustrated in the moving description of their farewell to Paul: 'When he had spoken thus, he knelt down and prayed with them all. And they all wept and embraced Paul and kissed him, sorrowing most of all because of the word he had spoken, that they should see his face no more. And they brought him to the ship' (Acts 20³⁶⁻³⁸).

Smyrna, now the internationally famous Izmir, was a busy seaport about fifty miles further up the coast, known for the last two hundred years as 'the fairest of the cities of Ionia', and second in importance only to Ephesus itself. Its sudden rise to fame after four centuries of insignificance makes it possible for John to greet its Christians in the name of the Christ 'who died and came to life', the eternal conqueror of death; and its reputation for loyalty to Rome (it had earned itself the title 'faithful') allows him to demand from them the same sort of fidelity to Christ, 'unto death'. Meanwhile he has nothing but sympathy for their sufferings. Reduced to penury and harassed, as Paul had been throughout his journeys in Asia, by Jewish jealousy, misrepresentation and false accusation,* they are not to lose heart: Jews who can treat their brethren in this way have forfeited their claim to be called Israel, the people of God.† They are no more than the agents of Satan, whom God will not allow to test his people overmuch or overlong.‡ Even if they have to die for it, those who persevere are assured of their reward: a 'wreath of life' more glorious than the 'wreath' which crowned Smyrna's eastern hill, an immortality which death would never be able to touch again.

3. Pergamum

2 ¹²And to the angel of the church in Pergamum write: 'The words of him who has the sharp two-edged sword.
¹³'I know where you dwell, where Satan's throne is; you hold fast to my name and you did not deny my faith even in the days of Antipas my witness, my faithful one, who was killed among you, where Satan dwells. ¹⁴But I have a few things against you: you have some there who hold the teaching of Balaam, who taught Balak to

* It was the same Jews who, fifty years later, were to instigate the pagans to howl for the death of Smyrna's bishop Polycarp.
† 'Israel' is the title which the rest of the New Testament would have used for those who have inherited the promises made by God in the Old Testament. The author of the Apocalypse strangely calls these 'Jews', a title which St John's Gospel always reserves for the opponents of Christianity.
‡ 'Ten days' would seem to be a symbol for a short time. See Gen. 24⁵⁵ of Rebekah's delay in her parents' home, and Dan. 1⁸⁻¹⁶ of Daniel's fast.

put a stumbling block before the sons of Israel, that they might eat food sacrificed to idols and practise immorality. [15]So you also have some who hold the teaching of the Nicolaitans. [16]Repent then. If not, I will come to you soon and war against them with the sword of my mouth. [17]He who has an ear, let him hear what the Spirit says to the churches. To him who conquers I will give some of the hidden manna, and I will give him a white stone, with a new name written on the stone which no one knows except him who receives it.'

Pergamum, the modern Bergama, lay another fifty miles further north, and was the centre from which Rome administered the province of Asia. Not surprisingly it was also the centre from which was propagated the emperor-worship which was such a convenient gauge of political loyalty, but which so revolted the author of the Apocalypse—for whom Caesar's claim to the divine title 'Lord' was something devilish, and the city which supported that claim was 'Satan's throne'. In this oppressive atmosphere, it is perhaps not to be wondered at that some Christians had waned in their singleminded adherence to Christ the Lord. John seems to be in full sympathy with their difficulties: 'I know where you dwell, where Satan's throne is.' Nevertheless he addresses them in the stern name of 'him who has the sharp two-edged sword', Christ the punisher of evil. Not that they had apostasized: they had probably done no more than take part in the city's social life by attending banquets where food previously used in pagan worship was served. St Paul had already come across the problem among his own converts in Corinth, and had given the most lenient of answers to the questions they put to him.* But in Pergamum the situation was different: this concession to pagan ways was being interpreted as an approval of pagan sacrifice. John can only call it 'immorality' (literally 'adultery' against the God with whom they had entered a marriage-covenant), and those Gnostic-minded Christians who advocated it he can only compare to the Balaam who in Moses' time had tempted God's People to the same 'adulterous' abandonment of God's demands.† By a piece

* See 1 Cor. 10[23-30].   † See Num. 31[16] and 25[1-3].

of punning typical of apocalyptic writings, it is this word Balaam which is probably the explanation of the name 'Nicolaitans' mentioned in reference to both Pergamum and Ephesus. Nicolas would not be the name of an actual person, but simply a cryptogram for Balaam,* who is himself a symbol for compromise with paganism.

Yet in spite of these strictures, John finds much to praise in the church at Pergamum. One of its Christians has already been put to death for holding fast to Christ's name of *Kyrios*—the Lord. Others will no doubt be called upon to bear the same supreme witness.† In a wealth of symbolism John promises them, in contrast with the idol-tainted foods he is asking them to forgo, a food which will give them the very life of God; and in contrast with the white counter which would have allowed them admission into the pagan feasts, an entrance ticket into heaven itself, inscribed with the name of the true and inalienable self which the Christian assumes in the kingdom of heaven.

4. Thyatira

2 ¹⁸And to the angel of the church in Thyatira write: 'The words of the Son of God, who has eyes like a flame of fire, and whose feet are like burnished bronze.

¹⁹'I know your works, your love and faith and service and patient endurance, and that your latter works exceed the first. ²⁰But I have this against you, that you tolerate the woman Jezebel, who calls herself a prophetess and is teaching and beguiling my servants to practise immorality and to eat food sacrificed to idols. ²¹I gave her time to repent, but she refuses to repent of her immorality. ²²Behold, I will throw her on a sickbed, and those who commit adultery with her I will throw into great tribulation, unless they repent of her doings; ²³and I will strike her children dead. And all the churches shall know that I am he who searches mind and heart, and I will give to each of you as your works deserve. ²⁴But to the rest of you in Thyatira, who do not hold this teaching, who have not learned what some call the deep things of Satan, to you I say, I do not lay

* In Hebrew the word Balaam can be made to mean 'He lords it over the people.' A rough Greek equivalent of this would be 'Nika laon'. If John had been writing for English readers, he might have called these liberal Christians 'Folklore(d)'.
† The Greek word for witness is 'martyr'.

upon you any other burden; [25]only hold fast what you have, until I come. [26]He who conquers and who keeps my works until the end, I will give him powers over the nations, [27]and he shall rule them with a rod of iron, as when earthen pots are broken in pieces, even as I myself have received power from my Father; [28]and I will give him the morning star. [29]He who has an ear, let him hear what the Spirit says to the churches.'

Thyatira, the modern Akhisar on the open plain between Pergamum and Sardis, was the least important of the seven cities to which the book is addressed. It was famous, however, for its guilds—would they be called trade unions today?—which so permeated the city's life* that the Christian community could scarcely have avoided being involved in them. At the lower levels these associations would not necessarily have interfered with the Christian life of their members. But the higher income groups must have found it difficult to reconcile their Christian beliefs with their business interests, closely tied up as these inevitably were with the patron gods of the various crafts.

John again shows himself sympathetic to their difficulties, and has Christ address them under the title of the searcher of minds and hearts, who knows the social ostracism that many of them have willingly accepted in order to remain true to their faith. But he knows too those who have taken refuge from their difficulties in a Gnostic† interpretation of Christianity, according to which those who had seen the light were emancipated from the moral standards demanded of others, and could with impunity attend the trade-banquets at which food from the temple-sacrifices were eaten. John had earlier referred to this compromise with paganism as the unfaithfulness of a modern Balaam. Here he calls it the adultery of a modern Jezebel.‡ and demands that the Christian community firmly repudiate this

* Records refer to guilds of bakers, brassworkers, clothiers, dyers, linenworkers, potters, shoemakers, tanners and woolworkers existing in Thyatira at this time.

† 'The deep things' referred to in v. 24 was a phrase used by the Gnostics for the esoteric knowledge they claimed to possess.

‡ The pagan queen who introduced so many of her pagan ways into Israel that its worship of God became almost indistinguishable from the worship of Baal. See 1 Kings 16[31] ff.

diluted form of Christianity. Its pressure on the community is clearly great, but no greater than the pressure which Christ himself had to undergo from the world. Those who resist it until he comes again, who hold fast to his teaching as the apostles have faithfully handed it down, can expect to share his fate, but also his glory. The quotation in v. 26-27 is from the messianic psalm 2, which St Paul maintained could be applied to Christ only from the time of his resurrection.* It was only then that Christ won his victory, rising like the morning star from the darkness to proclaim that the Day of the Lord had dawned. But the same victory belongs to the Christian who remains united to that Christ.

5. Sardis

3 ¹And to the angel of the church in Sardis write: 'The words of him who has the seven spirits of God and the seven stars.

"I know your works; you have the name of being alive, and you are dead. ²Awake, and strengthen what remains and is on the point of death, for I have not found your works perfect in the sight of my God. ³Remember then what you received and heard; keep that and repent. If you will not awake, I will come like a thief, and you will not know at what hour I will come upon you. ⁴Yet you have still a few names in Sardis, people who have not soiled their garments; and they shall walk with me in white, for they are worthy. ⁵He who conquers shall be clad thus in white garments, and I will not blot his name out of the book of life; I will confess his name before my Father and before his angels. ⁶He who has an ear, let him hear what the Spirit says to the churches.'

Sardis, capital city of the almost legendary Croesus and the financial leader of the ancient world,† had by New Testament times lost its proverbial glory and sunk into obscurity. John's complaint is that its Christian community seems to be repeating the same history and betraying its early promise of greatness. Its true glory, like that of Sardis, belongs to the past. Its present life is a sham, a feverish activity which hides the critical danger

* Acts 13³³, Rom. 1⁴.
† Pieces of silver from the seventh century B.C., stamped with the heads of kings of Sardis, are among the first known coins.

it is truly in. The message addressed to it comes aptly from the Christ who is the controller and supervisor of all the Church, and whose piercing gaze* has penetrated this complacent façade to reveal the death, or near-death, that lies behind it. John appeals to the Christians of Sardis to awake out of this torpor in order to salvage what little true Christian life remains, lest Christ in his imminent coming should catch them by surprise, as the city itself, complacent in its supposed impregnability, had twice in its history been unexpectedly overcome and sacked.† For only a handful of the community has he any praise, those who have been faithful to the Gospel message, and have kept themselves free from the deadly spirit which has defiled their brethren.‡ They alone, unless the warning is heeded, will be invested in the 'whiteness' which symbolizes the victory and joy of heaven, and inscribed on the 'registers' of heaven.

6. Philadelphia

3 ⁷And to the angel of the church in Philadelphia write: 'The words of the holy one, the true one, who has the key of David, who opens and no one shall shut, who shuts and no one opens.
⁸'I know your works. Behold, I have set before you an open door, which no one is able to shut; I know that you have but little power, and yet you have kept my word and have not denied my name. ⁹Behold, I will make those of the synagogue of Satan who say that they are Jews and are not, but lie—behold, I will make them come and bow down before your feet, and learn that I have loved you. ¹⁰Because you have kept my word of patient endurance, I will keep you from the hour of trial which is coming on the whole world, to try those who dwell upon the earth. ¹¹I am coming soon; hold fast what you have, so that no one may seize your crown. ¹²He who conquers, I will make him a pillar in the temple of my God; never shall he go out of it, and I will write on him the name of my God, and the name of the city of my God, the New Jerusalem which

---

* Christ's sevenfold Spirit, mentioned here, is in 5⁶ compared to the eyes with which he has knowledge of all things.

† Once by the Persian commander Cyrus in the sixth century B.C., and again in the third century by the Greek army of Antiochus the Great.

‡ Another topical reference. Sardis claimed to have been a pioneer in the art of wool-dying.

comes down from my God out of heaven, and my own new name. [13]He who has an ear, let him hear what the Spirit says to the churches.'

Philadelphia, today called Alaşehir, had been founded only two centuries earlier, as a centre for diffusing Greek culture to the Asian interior. Its Christians are addressed by the Christ who, as the keeper of the door which leads to life, has commissioned them to fulfil a similar missionary role in diffusing the Gospel. In spite of their poverty they have zealously carried out this commission, and John has nothing but praise for them in thus living out the implications of their acceptance of Christ as the 'Lord', the name by which the Roman emperor would have liked them to acknowledge him.* Nevertheless it is not from Rome that their difficulties have arisen. They are plagued, as Smyrna had been,† by the opposition of those who, by their rejection of the Christ who was the true fulfilment of Jewish hopes, have forfeited their right to the title 'Jew'. God's promises have been inherited by the new Israel of the Church, and John fortells that these Jewish critics will be forced to acknowledge this if they wish to become, like the Philadelphians, the living columns of that Temple which bears the name of New Jerusalem, and which, unlike Philadelphia's 'New Caesarea', will stand unmoveable for ever.‡

7. Laodicea

3 [14]And to the angel of the church in Laodicea write: 'The words of the Amen, the faithful and true witness, the beginning of God's creation.

[15]'I know your works: you are neither cold nor hot. Would that you were cold or hot! [16]So, because you are lukewarm, and neither cold nor hot, I will spew you out of my mouth. [17]For you say, I am rich, I have prospered, and I need nothing; not knowing that you

---

* So also in 2[3] and 2[13].

† See 2[9].

‡ Philadelphia suffered from frequent earth tremors. After the earthquake of A.D. 17, the city had to be largely reconstructed, and in honour of Tiberius Caesar who financed the project acquired the second name of Neocaesarea.

are wretched, pitiable, poor, blind and naked. [18]Therefore I counsel you to buy from me gold refined by fire, that you may be rich, and white garments to clothe you and to keep the shame of your naked-ness from being seen, and salve to anoint your eyes, that you may see. [19]Those whom I love, I reprove and chasten; so be zealous and repent. [20]Behold, I stand at the door and knock; if anyone hears my voice and opens the door, I will come in to him and eat with him, and he with me. [21]He who conquers, I will grant him to sit with me on my throne, as I myself conquered and sat down with my Father on his throne. [22]He who has an ear, let him hear what the Spirit says to the churches.'

Of Laodicea, the recipient of the fiercest of John's messages, nothing now remains except a few lonely ruins. In New Testament times it still lay on an important crossroad of the Roman Empire, and was known throughout the Mediterranean world as a centre of industry, commerce and banking, famous especially for its exports of eye ointment and black woollen cloth. Its citizens could in all truth congratulate themselves on the energy which had brought them prosperity and indepen-dence enough to be able, after the earthquake of the year 60, proudly to refuse the help offered them by Rome, and rebuild the city from their own resources.

Not surprisingly, such material well-being had not been echoed in the spiritual life of Laodicea's Christians.* John addresses them, vehemently, in the name of the Christ who is the Guarantor of God's Covenant,† with its threat of punish-ment as well as its promise of reward. Their proud and complacent self-satisfaction had bred in them a tepid half-heartedness which was more loathsome‡ than a frank rejection of their faith. As it was, they were neither one thing nor the other, and in imminent danger of being spat out of God's mouth in disgust. Yet John's final appeal to them is full of tenderness,

---

* The message to Smyrna in 2[9] had already pointed out that material and spiritual prosperity rarely go together.

† The word 'Amen', as was mentioned in reference to 1[8], comes from a root which means 'certainty', 'guaranteed reliability'. Christ, as the expression of God's faithfulness to his promise, is God's 'Amen' to the Covenant.

‡ The lukewarm springs of Hierapolis, with their nauseating odour of sulphur, lie directly opposite Laodicea, their overflow into the valley leaving on its cliffs a white mineral deposit which can be seen for miles around.

for the reproof he has administered has been aroused not by hatred but by love. Christ's only desire, as their elder brother and the source of all their happiness,* is to enter into intimate union with them, and he waits only for an opportunity to prove it. To those who answer his invitation he promises a share in his own victory on the 'throne' which is to occupy the centre of the next vision.

It should be clear by now that each of the sections we have studied in this chapter is parallel with the others. While mutually completing each other, they have all individually stated the same theme, using a system of recapitulation which is going to be common to the whole book. The different titles of Christ all ultimately mean the same thing, and the different rewards that are promised to the various communities are not really distinct from each other at all.

It would be a pity, therefore, to restrict the different messages too narrowly to the various Christian communities to which they were first addressed, as if only Ephesus (but not Smyrna or Pergamum) stood in danger of having its lampstand removed, or only Sardis (but not Philadelphia or Laodicea) could look forward to being robed in white. John has indeed made the most intricate use of topical references, but these are only the setting for the message, which is intended to be taken to heart by all to whom it applies. The message accuses and judges and promises in terms of local geography and contemporary history. But its application is not local or temporary. It applies in some measure to each of the seven churches, and therefore to any subsequent readers of this covering letter.

The impressions which this prologue to the book leaves with us may be summed up as follows. The Christian communities to whom it is addressed are labouring under the most crushing of difficulties. Within these bustling, cultured and wealthy towns, they form tiny, almost insignificant groups, made up mostly of the poorer classes. Indeed, any rich person wishing to

* See verses 14 and 18.

join these groups would find that his conversion left him impov-
erished. Their faith cuts them off almost entirely from the
social life of their fellow townsmen, and on all sides there is
intense pressure upon them to conform. If some of them lapsed
from their faith, or relaxed their hold on it, it should not cause
us any surprise. The wonder is that any Christianity survived
at all. All the letters indicate that it did, and that a strong nucleus
remained faithful in each town.

Of John the author, the impression given is one of tremendous
authority combined with the most tender love. He is as inflexible
as the John of the Gospel and the epistles. Yet he has, too, a
passionate concern for the communities to which he is writing.
He knows exactly what each of the churches is going through,
and every letter speaks of the compassion he feels for them: 'I
know your works, your toil and your patient endurance . . . I
know your tribulation and your poverty (but you are rich) . . . I
know that you have but little power . . . I know where you
dwell, where Satan's throne is.'

But the most lasting impression of all is of the majesty of the
Christ whom John proposes as the answer to their anguish.
This is no mawkish or milksop Christ, but someone before
whom John falls down as dead, 'the Alpha and the Omega, the
Source of all creation and its Amen, whose word is a fiery
sword, whose hand holds masterfully all spirits . . . eternal
Power, eternal Wisdom, thrilling Omnipresence.'* If the
Fourth Gospel stresses Christ's divinity more than any of the
other Gospels or the epistles, what shall we say of this? And yet,
still as in the Fourth Gospel, this Christ is not in some remote
heaven, but moving about among his churches, present with
them in their suffering, the utterly human friend who sacrificed
himself for his friends, and who even now invites them into the
closest intimacy with him. The same figure, before whose
awe-inspiring majesty John falls prostrate, lays his right hand
upon him and says: 'Fear not . . . I stand at the door and knock;
if any one opens the door, I will come in to him and eat with

* Martindale, *op. cit.* p. 49-50.

him, and he with me.' The Christian is not sent on some remote mission far from Christ. He is a column built into the very Temple which is Christ.

Did anyone ask whether the Apocalypse has any relevance for the Christian of today? 'He who has an ear, let him hear what the Spirit says to the Church.'

III THE REVELATION

Chapters 4 to 21

The three chapters studied above detach themselves easily enough from the rest of the book. Anyone can see that they form an introduction to the work. Chapter 4 begins the Apocalypse proper, that is to say the 'Revelation', or 'unveiling' of a future which until now has been God's secret, but which the reader is now going to share through the visions granted to John. It is from chapter 4 that John is going to make seven distinct attempts to reveal this secret.

Before we approach the text, it will be a good thing to recall again some of the principles which we laid down earlier in reference to apocalyptic literature in general. And the first of these is that apocalyptic is a literary form, with its own rules and conventions. These an author must obey if he wishes to write a piece of apocalyptic. In other words, the reader has to understand from the beginning that the standpoint from which he is being asked to view things is a fictional one, not necessarily a real one. The principal fiction used by all apocalypses is the one which transports writer and reader into a pretended past. If something that is already known is to be presented as if it were a great secret—and that is the whole supposition—then it cannot be done in any other way than by pretending to see it before it has happened. This means that the book's future tenses are not necessarily future to the author or the reader; they should in reality be past and present. But if it was an accepted literary convention in this kind of writing, to put them into the future, then there is no reason why John should not do the same. When he speaks, therefore, of 'that which is to come', we do not necessarily have to look beyond his times for its fulfilment.

Consequently the visions themselves are not necessarily real ones. Of course, it is quite possible that John stands right outside the ranks of all other apocalyptists. But none of *them* had any scruples about expressing their convictions in a series of fictitious visions, which were the stock-in-trade of the apocalyptic writer, and if John chose to write in their literary form there is no reason why he should not have made use of their patrimony. It should cause us no surprise to find close parallels, in both the Old Testament and contemporary apocalyptic writings, for most of the ideas and symbols in which John clothes the visions he wishes to describe.

It would be a mistake, therefore, to try to visualize these visions. The elements of which they have been made up are often inconsistent with each other. One has been superimposed on top of another in a way which makes them quite unimaginable. The various symbols have been borrowed for the meaning that they contain, and the reader is meant to go immediately to this meaning, and not remain enmeshed in the problem of what the symbols would have looked like. There is no purpose served in trying to work out (as some commentators in the past have done) the geography of these visions, to ask for instance where the throne would stand in relation to the rest of the things mentioned, or where exactly the twenty-four elders are to be fitted in, or how they are able to fall on their faces in 4^{10} without upsetting the bowls of incense they are holding in 5^8. The throne is not a piece of furniture: it is meant to evoke the idea of majesty and judgment. The prostration of the elders is not an acrobatic feat: it is meant to express the idea of homage. It is the idea which must be seized, even though John has decided to convey it in visual terms.

The Lamb (*chapters* 4 *to* 5)

What has just been said must be qualified at once, at least in reference to the first two chapters, the visual character of which is overwhelmingly rich. We have said that the reader must mortify his imagination, but not to the extent that he misses the artistry that has gone into the making of this vision, with its exquisite use of colours and its arresting technique of presenting first of all the central figure, and then slowly revealing what surrounds him, in ever widening circles. The technique is rather like that of the TV camera which begins a scene on a close-up and then gradually moves backwards. John had never heard of television, but he gets exactly the same effect by asking the reader to imagine a door, and asking him to approach it closer and closer to be able to see more and more of what lies behind its frame.

1. The Throne

4 ¹After this I looked, and lo, in heaven an open door! And the first voice, which I had heard speaking to me like a trumpet, said, 'Come up hither, and I will show you what must take place after this.' ²At once I was in the Spirit, and lo, a throne stood in heaven, with one seated on the throne! ³And he who sat there appeared like jasper and carnelian, and round the throne was a rainbow that looked like an emerald. ⁴Round the throne were twenty-four thrones, and seated on the thrones were twenty-four elders, clad in white garments, with golden crowns upon their heads. ⁵From the throne issue flashes of lightning, and voices and peals of thunder, and before the throne burn seven torches of fire, which are the seven spirits of God; ⁶and before the throne there is as it were a sea of glass, like crystal.

And round the throne, on each side of the throne, are four living creatures, full of eyes in front and behind: ⁷the first living creature like a lion, the second living creature like an ox, the third living creature with the face of a man, and the fourth living creature like a flying eagle. ⁸And the four living creatures, each of them with six wings, are full of eyes all round and within, and day and night they never cease to sing,

'Holy, holy, holy, is the Lord God Almighty,
who was and is and is to come!'

[9]And whenever the living creatures give glory and honour and thanks to him who is seated on the throne, who lives for ever and ever, [10]the twenty-four elders fall down before him who is seated on the throne and worship him who lives for ever and ever; they cast their crowns before the throne, singing,

> [11]'Worthy art thou, our Lord and God,
> to receive glory and honour and power,
> for thou didst create all things,
> and by thy will they existed and were created.'

We start then, at the very centre of the picture, with the throne, and seated upon it, 'One', an indescribable 'Someone'.* It is worth remarking that this book, which is otherwise so free in its imagery, nowhere makes any attempt to describe this central Figure. It is a master-touch thus to convey the inexpressible and supreme mystery that is God, whom no one can see. The only thing of him that can be seen is his Glory, that dazzling light which surrounds him in order to reveal him and hide him at the same time. If one must describe him, one can only do so in terms of that brilliant and multicoloured light: 'A throne stood in heaven . . . and he who sat there appeared like jasper and carnelian . . . a rainbow that looked like an emerald.' The terms are borrowed from Ezekiel, where a similar attempt is made to describe the indescribable:

> Above the firmament . . . there was the likeness of a throne, in appearance like sapphire; and seated above the likeness of a throne was a likeness as it were of a human form. And . . . I saw as it were gleaming bronze, like the appearance of fire . . . and there was brightness round about him. Like the appearance of the bow that is in the cloud on the day of rain, so was the appearance of the brightness round about. Such was the appearance of the likeness of the glory of the Lord. And when I saw it, I fell upon my face.†

For all the care taken by Ezekiel to preserve God's unutterable mystery by the repeated use of 'like', 'as it were', 'likeness', 'appearance', John has succeeded better than he. In simplifying Ezekiel's picture, he has purified it still more and not even

* The last vision of the book finishes with the same central Figure seated upon the throne. See 21[5], 22[1,3].
† Ezek. 1[26-28].

allowed God to be thought of in terms of a human figure. God remains utterly transcendent and unimaginable.

The flashes of lightning and peals of thunder that issue from the throne are similarly borrowed from the Old Testament where, from the time of the theophany on mount Sinai onwards, the awe-inspiring elements of a storm are regularly used as a symbol for announcing the presence of God.* So too is the 'sea' upon which the whole scene is set. For the Hebrew, working only upon what he could see, the earth was flat and supported by pillars upon the oceans of water that surrounded it. What kept these waters separated from the snow, hail and rain-water above was the firmament, which was conceived of as a solid vault supporting and restraining that other sea of water. It was above those waters that God dwelt, in his own heaven, inaccessible and transcendent.†

With that central theme of the throne fixed, the reader is brought closer to the 'door' to see the twenty-four elders who surround the throne, and closer still to see in detail the living creatures that stand at its four corners. These provide a good example of the need to recognize John's symbols for what they are, and to translate them directly into intelligible terms. We do not have to imagine that heaven *looks* like this. We do not even have to find an actual reality corresponding to these twenty-four and those four. The reader is meant simply to recognize the place from which John has borrowed these symbols, and immediately see their significance.

The twenty-four elders John has borrowed from the Jerusalem temple. There the priests were divided into twenty-four classes or orders, each headed by a priest referred to as 'chief man' or 'officer',‡ and later as 'senior' or 'elder'.§ The fact that they are clothed in white and are later said to offer up the incense which is the prayer of the faithful‖ makes it quite clear

* See Exod. 19¹⁶, Jud. 5⁴, Ps. 18⁸⁻¹⁶, 97³⁻⁵, etc.

† The same idea lay behind the provision of a 'sea' of water in front of the inner sanctuary of the Temple, where God had condescended to make his dwelling on earth. See 1 Kings 7²³⁻²⁶.

‡ 1 Chron. 24¹⁻¹⁹.   § 2 Kings 19².   ‖ See 5⁸.

that this is what John has in mind. After all, if he wished to describe the 'heavenly liturgy', in what other terms could he do so but in those of the earthly liturgy he knew so well? Indeed, since the book of Isaiah had already described the heavenly court in terms of a God surrounded by his elders,* it would seem that John did not have to invent the symbol. It had already become part of the conventional apocalyptic imagery.

The four living creatures are similarly borrowed figures, again mainly from Ezekiel:

> In the midst of the fire . . . came the likeness of four living creatures. . . . Each had four faces, and each of them had four wings. Their legs were straight, and the soles of their feet were like the sole of a calf's foot. . . . Each had the face of a man in front; the four had the face of a lion on the right side, the four had the face of an ox on the left side, and the four had the face of an eagle at the back. . . . Each creature had two wings, each of which touched the wing of another, while two covered their bodies. . . .
>
> Now as I looked at the living creatures, I saw a wheel upon the earth beside the living creatures, one for each of the four of them. . . . The four wheels had rims and they had spokes; and their rims were full of eyes round about. And when the living creatures went, the wheels went beside them . . . for the spirit of the living creatures was in the wheels.†

This page of Ezekiel was itself a mystery until archaeology came to our aid.‡ They are later called Cherubim, and would seem to represent Ezekiel's impression of the sphinx-like 'Karibu' which have been dug out of the Mesopotamian soil in their dozens to grace the Assyrian Room of our principal museums. Their four 'faces' are really four aspects, since they each have a human face, the body of a bull, a lion's mane and eagles' wings. They were a regular feature of the Babylonian scene, where they were to be found in pairs before the entrance to palaces and temples, as the guardians of the king or the god. Ezekiel, writing from Babylon, uses these Babylonian figures in his

---

* Isa. 24²³, part of one of the later additions to the work of Isaiah, known commonly as the Apocalypse of Isaiah.

† Ezek. 1⁴⁻²¹.

‡ The rabbis said that it was beyond human powers to visualize, and forbade anyone to read it until he had reached the age of thirty.

vision because he wants to evoke a picture of the throne of God; and he puts it on wheels because, as he insists throughout his opening chapters, this God is not someone confined to the remote fastness of Jerusalem, but one who has come to Babylon to be present in the midst of the exiles.

This, then, has been the principal source on which John has drawn for his four living creatures, although he has again simplified his source by turning the original four aspects into four creatures with one aspect each. But he has gone to other sources too: to the book of Isaiah, where the inaugural vision features the winged Seraphim, who hide their faces and bodies in sacred fear of God's presence, and sing in praise of the Holy One, the King of tremendous majesty;* and to the Jewish apocalypses, where two other orders of angels regularly appear alongside the Cherubim and Seraphim—the Egregoroi who never close their eyes, and the Ophanim who are covered back and front, inside and out, with eyes.† The apocalyptic writers who make use of these four orders of divine attendants distinguish them carefully from each other and specify the duties that belong to each. John refuses to enter into this kind of speculation, and once again simplifies his material by combining Cherubim, Seraphim, Egregoroi and Ophanim into one order. But all his sources have contributed towards the effect for which he has used them: to evoke the overwhelming majesty and supremacy of God.

Scholars have gone into long disquisitions about the meaning of the elders and the living creatures. Do the twenty-four elders represent the twelve apostles alongside the twelve patriarchs, that is to say the New Testament Church alongside the Old, the new and the old Israel enthroned as judges in the presence of God? Do the four living creatures represent the four directions (north, south, east and west) or the four compartments (heaven, sea, earth and underworld) of the universe 'ever wakeful, ever

* See Isa. 6$^{1-5}$.

† Egregoroi (Greek) means Wideawake. The word Ophanim (Hebrew) means Wheels, and seems to be a further development of Ezekiel's vision.

consciously wanting and worshipping its God'?* In that case the whole of nature and the whole of the Church would be represented in this picture.† But these speculations seem to go somewhat beyond John's own terms of reference. Is it necessary to find something that the twenty-four and the four actually correspond to? Given the sources from which John has borrowed them, is it not sufficient to see them simply as symbols that convey something about *God*? If we like, we can say that this chapter offers us a description of the celestial court and the celestial hierarchy offering their praises to God. But all that John is saying is that God is a God of infinite holiness and infinite majesty.

The song of praise put into the mouth of the four living creatures

'Holy, holy, holy, is the Lord God Almighty,
who was and is and is to come!'

is taken from the same verses of Isaiah from which the details on the Seraphim were borrowed. It has been adapted into an exclamation of wonder at God's eternity, especially the future eternity towards which the book is focused. The song of praise put into the mouth of the twenty-four elders

They cast their crowns before the throne, singing,
'Worthy art thou, our Lord and God,
to receive glory and honour and power.'

is another protest against the prevalent emperor cult, which demanded this gesture of submission from vassal kings, and

---

* Martindale, *op. cit.* p. 54.

† Numerous other identifications have been proposed for the man, lion, bull and eagle that are mentioned in reference to the living creatures: the greatest of all creatures, of all wild beasts, of all domestic beasts, and of all birds; or what is wisest, noblest, strongest and swiftest in creation; or man as the tamer of nature's three wildest animals, and so the king of all creation; or the four qualities of Christ as Man, King, Priest and Dispenser of the Spirit; or the four evangelists Matthew (who begins his Gospel with Christ's human genealogy), Mark (who begins with a voice crying in the wilderness like a lion's), Luke (who begins with the temple and its memories of the sacrifice of bulls), and John (who begins by soaring into the heights of contemplation like an eagle). All the suggestions are equally arbitrary.

these acclamations and titles* from its devotees. John is saying, as he has said so many times already, that this homage, these acclamations and these titles belong to the Creator alone. For the Roman emperor to claim them is a blasphemy which the Christian must resist to the very end.

2. The Scroll

So far we have not moved out of the Old Testament. A Jew could have written that first part of the vision. But what follows can only come from the New Testament. For John has not yet finished with his vision of heaven. He takes another close-up:

> 5 ¹And I saw in the right hand of him who was seated on the throne a scroll written within and on the back, sealed with seven seals; ²and I saw a strong angel proclaiming with a loud voice, 'Who is worthy to open the scroll and break its seals?' ³And no one in heaven or on earth or under the earth was able to open the scroll or to look into it, ⁴and I wept much that no one was found worthy to open the scroll or to look into it. ⁵Then one of the elders said to me, 'Weep not; lo, the Lion of the tribe of Judah, the Root of David, has conquered, so that he can open the scroll and its seven seals.'

A book or a scroll is a prop common to all apocalyptic writers for conveying the revelation of a secret.† John has again borrowed this detail from Ezekiel, even down to the specification that it contained so much material that it could not all be fitted on one side of the parchment.‡ And he has again transformed it. For Ezekiel, the scroll was concrete expression of the divine punishment he was commissioned to preach. For John it contains, more significantly, the whole of God's secret plans, and it is to become the centrepiece of the vision he will describe in chapters 6-7.

Now those divine plans are secret because they have not yet taken place. They are said to be sealed with 'seven' seals to

---

* As was mentioned above, the emperor Domitian demanded to be addressed specifically as 'Lord and God'.

† Christian art generally represents it in the form of a volume which opens piece by piece. As our translation makes clear, John is thinking rather of a scroll, which cannot be opened at all until all its seals are broken.

‡ See Ezek. 2⁹⁻¹⁰.

convey the fact that they are a complete enigma, known to no one. The reader is supposed to get a feeling that he is going to be granted a peep into the future. But as was explained above, that future is largely a fiction. What an apocalypse really reveals is something that has already happened. The sealed scroll will be found to contain not simply the future, but the whole of history, future present and past. The past, especially, of the Old 'Testament', for that is the word that would be conjured up in the mind of the Christian by the mention of seven seals: Roman law demanded that a last will and Testament should be sealed by seven witnesses, and that it could not be executed before all seven seals were broken. John is presenting his scroll as a divine Testament, whose content remained a mystery until the coming of Christ.

In this, he follows very closely the thought of the prophets. Isaiah had complained bitterly that Israel did not see the point of its own Scriptures,* and the complaint was echoed frequently in the accusation that the people were blind to the meaning of a history in which God had revealed his plans to those who had the eyes to see it. The task of the prophets was precisely to meditate on Israel's history and on their own records of it in order to show men how God's plans were contained in it. The later prophets were even content simply to take up the words of their predecessors, and repeat them insistently with the invitation to 'hear the Word of the Lord.' Christ himself claimed to be the last of that line of prophets, and as the Word of God made flesh, he could only point to himself as the final revelation to mankind of God's plans. To turn one's back on him was to turn one's back on all that God had tried to tell us of himself. In the same spirit St Paul reproaches his fellow Jews in the very words used by the prophets before him: 'To this day, when they read the Old Covenant (Testament), that same veil remains unlifted, because only through Christ is it taken away.

* 'The vision of all this has become to you like the words of a book that is sealed. When men give it to one who can read, saying, "Read this," he says, "I cannot, for it is sealed." And when they give the book to one who cannot read, saying, "Read this," he says, "I cannot read" ' (Isa. 29[11–12]).

Yes, to this day whenever Moses is read a veil lies over their minds; but when a man turns to the Lord the veil is removed.'*

This is what John would have in mind when he writes that he 'wept much that no one was found worthy to open the scroll or to look into it'. This is no dream sequence in which one weeps out of sheer frustration. It is an echo of the anguish felt by the whole of first century Christianity, unable to understand the persecution it was undergoing. Nor was it only present events that Christians thought they could not understand or control. The whole of history, past as well as present, would remain an enigma to them as long as they forgot the Christ who, as the 'Lion of Judah and the Root of David', was able to open the scroll.

Both are messianic titles taken from the Old Testament. The first comes from the famous oracle in which the patriarch Jacob is represented as foretelling the destiny of the twelve tribes of Israel, and granting supremacy over the others to Judah, the 'lion' among the other animals.† The oracle was composed with David of Judah in mind, but it was taken up after his death and applied to the Messiah who, as a second David, would complete the work he had left unfinished. The 'root' metaphor is more directly messianic, being taken from the passages in the Old Testament which compare David's dynasty to a tree, tragically cut down at the time of the Babylonian exile, but destined to send out a new shoot which would revive its ancient glory. The most famous of these passages occurs in the prophet Isaiah, who includes in the promise a mention of the sevenfold Spirit, which John will take up in a moment:

> There shall come forth a shoot from the stump of Jesse,
> and a branch shall grow out of his roots.
> And the Spirit of the Lord shall rest upon him,
> the Spirit of wisdom and understanding,
> the Spirit of counsel and might,
> the Spirit of knowledge and the fear of the Lord.‡

---

* 2 Cor. 3[14-16].   † See Gen. 49[9-10].

‡ Isa. 11[1-2]. The Greek version, which John would have used and which is followed by the Latin Vulgate and those translations taken from it, adds as a seventh 'the Spirit of piety'.

According to the New Testament, these messianic titles (among others) were conferred on Christ in their fullness at the moment of his resurrection. The first preaching of the Christian message outlined in the Acts of the Apostles even goes so far as to say that Jesus 'became' the Christ or Messiah in his resurrection.* For the resurrection was seen not simply as the unexpected reversal of what would otherwise have been a tragedy, but as the whole purpose of Christ's work. He had come to overcome death, to break this final stranglehold that sin had on mankind. In his resurrection, Christ achieved what he had come to do. This was the Messiah's task, and this was where he proved himself to be the Messiah.

What John is therefore suggesting in these lines—and he will make it even more explicit in a moment—is that it is Christ alone, through his victory over death, who can open the scroll of the divine Testament. In other words, the resurrection is itself the key not only to the whole of the secret future, but to the whole of the past as well. It is the explanation of the entire plan of God. St Luke had expressed the same thought in his picture of the risen Christ revealing to his disciples the meaning of the Old Testament: 'Beginning with Moses and all the prophets, he interpreted to them in all the Scriptures the things concerning himself.'† The Church expresses the same thought in the Easter Vigil, where the Old Testament lessons are read by the light of the Easter Candle. The Old Testament remains an unintelligible enigma until it is read in the light of the risen Christ. His resurrection is the complete explanation, opening all its seven seals. We shall return to this subject later.

3. The Lamb

The final section of this first vision simply makes this thought of John more precise:

> 5 ⁶And between the throne and the four living creatures and among the elders, I saw a Lamb standing, as though it had been slain,

---

* Acts 2³⁶. See also Rom. 1⁴.   † See Luke 24²⁵⁻²⁷.

with seven horns and with seven eyes, which are the seven spirits of God sent out into all the earth; [7]and he went and took the scroll from the right hand of him who was seated on the throne. [8]And when he had taken the scroll, the four living creatures and the twenty-four elders fell down before the Lamb, each holding a harp, and with golden bowls full of incense, which are the prayers of the saints; [9]and they sang a new song, saying,

'Worthy art thou to take the scroll and to open its seals,
for thou wast slain and by thy blood didst ransom men for God
from every tribe and tongue and people and nation,
[10]and hast made them a kingdom and priests to our God,
and they shall reign on earth.'

[11]Then I looked, and I heard around the throne and the living creatures and the elders the voice of many angels, numbering myriads of myriads and thousands of thousands, [12]saying with a loud voice, 'Worthy is the Lamb who was slain, to receive power and wealth and wisdom and might and honour and glory and blessing!' [13]And I heard every creature in heaven and in earth and under the earth and in the sea, and all therein, saying, 'To him who sits upon the throne and to the Lamb be blessing and honour and glory and might for ever and ever!' [14]And the four living creatures said, 'Amen!' and the elders fell down and worshipped.

This passage provides another example of how each symbol must be translated immediately into the intellectual terms for which it stands. A Lamb cannot be superimposed on a Lion, nor a dead Lamb on a living Lamb. Visually the ideas are incompatible. It is the meaning of each that must be seized. Yet John has deliberately used this visual contradiction to emphasize the unexpected character of Christ's messianity. The Old Testament had hoped for a Lion. What the New Testament presents is a Lamb. What men had hoped for was a Messiah in glory. What they were given was a man nailed on a cross. Yet that ignominious death did not preclude a resurrection in glory: the Lamb is at once slain and living.*

* It is interesting that of all four Gospels it is, again, the Fourth that lays most emphasis on the apparent contradiction between Lion and Lamb, and between death and resurrection. It is St John alone who insists that the resurrection cannot be separated from the crucifixion, nor the crucifixion from the resurrection. The cross is itself already the glorification of Christ (Jn. 12[20–33]), and the risen Christ is still able to show his wounds (Jn. 20[27]). There is an obvious link between this last scene and the picture here given of the Lamb slain, yet standing and moving.

The figure of the Lamb has been taken from the Fourth Gospel, where it is more than a symbol of innocence, or an allusion to the Suffering Servant, innocent as 'a lamb that is led to the slaughter'.* It is a reference to the Passover lamb which was sacrificed to mark the liberation of Israel and their passing over from the slavery of Egypt to the freedom of the Promised Land. This Passover theme, which the evangelist saw fulfilled to perfection in Christ's life, especially at the moment of his death,† is clearly in our author's mind here also, as will be shown presently. For him, Christ is the Lamb because he effected the redemption of God's People: through his death and resurrection he liberated them from their slavery and brought them into the Kingdom of God. It is because of that victory that he is described here as having seven horns, that is to say the plenitude of power.

And also, through his seven eyes, the plenitude of knowledge. For these eyes, John explains, are the sevenfold Spirit which it was his messianic task to pour out upon men. This task too he fulfilled in his resurrection, when he became in all fullness the Spirit-impregnated Messiah.‡ It is through these 'eyes' that he continues now to be present with his followers, seeing them as they see him, in his Spirit.§

---

* Isa. 53[7].

† John 19[36] quotes the actual rubric governing the sacrifice of the Passover lamb, 'Not a bone of him shall be broken' (Exod. 12[46]), and sees it fulfilled in Christ's death.

‡ See the reference above to Isa. 11[1-2].

§ This seven-fold Spirit, which is said in 1[4] and 4[5] to stand before the throne of God like a sevenfold flame of fire, and in 3[1] and 5[6] to belong to Christ like a sevenfold eye (1[14] also compares Christ's eyes to a flame of fire), is explained by many commentators as a reference to seven unspecified angels. At first sight this explanation would seem easier to accept. But the resurrection-context of 5[6] would seem to indicate that for John the 'seven spirits' are to be understood as a description of the Holy Spirit. In this, he again comes very close to the theology of the Fourth Gospel, where the resurrection is also not only a demonstration of Christ's victory, but the occasion of his 'giving up his Spirit' (John 19[30]). In fact, according to the evangelist, it was not until Christ was glorified that he could complete his task of sending forth his Spirit on those who believed in him (7[39]), and so be with them always in order to unite them to his Father in heaven (14[16-20]).

As this symbol of the risen Christ is revealed, the whole hierarchy of heaven bursts out into a song of praise—no longer, as before, of him who is seated on the throne, but of the Lamb. It is called a 'new song', but as the context makes clear, what it celebrates is not a new theme, but the new application of the age-old theme of the Exodus.* This reality had indeed already been repeated and driven deeper many times in Israel's history, and greeted with a 'new song'.† But the new song sung here is as final as the new name and the new Jerusalem mentioned earlier, and the new Heaven and Earth with which the book will conclude. For Christ's resurrection is not simply a pledge of salvation still to come. It *is* salvation. By it, God's people have already become the Kingdom of God, and are here and now reigning‡ on earth. The original readers of this chapter might well have asked themselves, 'How?' Surely it was Caesar and his provincial representatives who had the upper hand! They would understand better, as we shall, by reading on. But it is as well to realize at this point that it was John's purpose to persuade them that the Kingdom was a present reality.

Still using his camera-technique, John finally moves further back to take in an even wider view. The song of praise of the heavenly hierarchy is taken up by the whole court of heaven, who in their seven acclamations wish to pour out upon Christ the plenitude of praise which they had previously given to God alone. In the last verses, this perspective opens wider still to allow the whole of creation to take up the praise, to which heaven can only give its *Amen* of agreement.§

---

* The words 'ransom', 'kingdom' and 'priests' are taken from the description of the first Exodus, where Israel had become a kingdom of priests, devoted entirely to the service of God. See Exod. 6⁶, 19⁶.

† See Pss. 33³, 96¹, 98¹, 144⁹, 149¹, Isa. 42¹⁰.

‡ The better Greek text of v. 10 reads the present tense, not the future.

§ The divinity of Christ is nowhere in the New Testament so clearly presented as in these songs, which address him in the same terms as previous chapters had insisted were reserved for God alone. The letters of Pliny, which are contemporary with the publication of this book and which express such astonishment that the Christians of his province should 'carmen Christo quasi *deo* dicere', would be referring to songs like these.

With that, John completes his first statement of a theme which he will repeat six times more. If each of his symbols is translated as it is given, its meaning is clear. The supreme control of the universe is in the hands of God, and it is shared on earth not by the Caesars of this world but by Christ, who achieved this supremacy in a death and resurrection which was the climax of God's plans in the past, and the revelation of his plans for the future. This fact is already acknowledged in the *Sanctus* of heaven, and by showing us the whole of creation also acknowledging it with its *Gloria*,* John has already told us the end of the story. One could say, as some commentators do, that this first vision is meant to provide an unchanging background to the rest of the book. But the same could be said of any of the other visions, which will simply repeat, in a different but parallel form, the lesson of the first: that the Christ who has won his victory in the past, has won it for all time, particularly for the present in which the reader is living.

The Sevens (*chapters* 6-11 *and* 15-16)

St Jerome, writing about the Apocalypse in one of his many letters to his friends, makes the observation that it has as many mysteries as it has words. He adds: 'That is putting it mildly; there are dozens of mysteries in each word.'† If that remark can be applied to John's first vision, it applies with a vengeance to the three series of seven which follow, the seven seals, the seven trumpets and the seven bowls of wrath. All is not darkness however. It will become obvious as we go that each series is complete in itself, expressing the whole theme, not simply part of it. Not that these series are entirely isolated from each other. One will easily take up and develop ideas which have been expressed previously: indeed, the first of the sevens is precisely a further elaboration of one of the secondary details of the first vision, the seals. But the series are not meant to be read as if

---

* The apt comment is, again, from Martindale, *op. cit.* p. 56.
† *Ep.* 53 *ad Paulinum*, PL 22. 548-549.

they were in sequence with each other, as if twenty-one different things had to be identified before we were sure that our interpretation was the right one. Each series is a complete statement of John's theme, starting at the beginning and finishing at the end. This is suggested not only by the use of the number seven (which in apocalyptic language already means totality) but also by the way in which these sevens are built up. They all begin with four of a kind, to which three other things are added. These last three are split into two plus one, the last always being delayed by the insertion of some apparently extraneous material in order to heighten the reader's interest and convince him that when the seventh finally arrives, it is the end to which nothing more can be added.*

1. The Seven Seals

The vision of ch. 4-5 has already explained to us what the seven-sealed scroll stands for: it is the whole of history, Old Testament and New, whose meaning remains a secret until the seals are broken. Since the scroll cannot be read at all until all seven have been broken, the gradual opening of one after the other cannot strictly be said to reveal to us different pieces of history. It is obviously a dramatic device to catch the attention of the reader, and convince him that the final secret is soon to be revealed.

The four of a kind in this, the first of our sevens, are the famous four horsemen of the apocalypse.

6 [1]Now I saw when the Lamb opened one of the seven seals, and I heard one of the four living creatures say, as with a voice of thunder,

---

* These sevens have given such a clear shape to the chapters here being discussed that some commentators have tried to find a similar 'seven-pattern' in the remaining chapters 12-14 and 17-20. An example may be seen in work of Martindale quoted above, pp. 19-21. The subdivisions required, as Martindale himself admits, are not very convincing, especially since they sometimes overlap with the other more clearly marked sevens. But what these attemps are searching for is real enough—a confirmation of the fact that each section will stand on its own, as a complete ('seven') statement of the theme of this book.

'Come!' ²And I saw, and behold, a white horse, and its rider had a bow; and a crown was given to him, and he went out conquering and to conquer.

³When he opened the second seal, I heard the second living creature say, 'Come!' ⁴And out came another horse, bright red; its rider was permitted to take peace from the earth, so that men should slay one another; and he was given a great sword.

⁵When he opened the third seal, I heard the third living creature say, 'Come!' And I saw, and behold, a black horse, and its rider had a balance in his hand; ⁶and I heard what seemed to be a voice in the midst of the four living creatures saying, 'A quart of wheat for a denarius, and three quarts of barley for a denarius; but do not harm oil and wine!'

⁷When he opened the fourth seal, I heard the voice of the fourth living creature say, 'Come!' ⁸And I saw, and behold, a pale horse, and its rider's name was Death, and Hades followed him.

Throughout this book, the colour white stands for victory. Red, the colour of blood, stands for violence and war, black for famine, and a pale colour—literally greenish white, the colour of decay—stands for plague and pestilence. It is therefore a quartet of conquest, war, famine and plague which is being described here, and in the final verse they are

6 ⁸given power over a fourth of the earth, to kill with sword and with famine and with pestilence and by wild beasts of the earth.

In ch. 19 the victorious horseman in white is Christ himself. But obviously this is not the case here, where the conquering forces are as unwelcome as the death and grave which follow them. One thinks more readily of the Parthians, whose army of sharpshooting bowmen was always feared by Rome. The famine that follows in their wake is vividly portrayed by the specification about the price of bread. A denarius, which is mentioned in the Gospels* as a day's wage for a labourer, and which normally bought thirteen quarts of wheat, here buys only one. the amount a man would eat in a day. In other words, we are talking of bare subsistence level, and famine prices. The

* In the parable of the labourers in the vineyard, Matt. 20¹⁻¹⁶.

command to be sparing with the wine and oil seems to be another comment on the same scarcity.*

The picture of four horsemen sent out to execute punishment on the four corners of the earth is taken from the Old Testament.† But John is not simply talking of punishment in general. He has described the four precisely in terms of those things which Christ in his eschatological discourse said would precede the 'coming of the Son of Man' and the 'End':

> When you hear of wars and rumours of wars, do not be alarmed; this must take place, but the End is not yet. For nation will rise against nation, and kingdom against kingdom; there will be earthquakes in various places, there will be famines; this is but the beginning of the sufferings.‡

In other words, John like Christ sees the last times being ushered in by a quartet of conquest, war, famine and plague. Does he leave it unspecified when they will come? Or is he thinking of events that had already taken place when he was writing—the defeat of the Roman legions by the Parthians in the year 62, the bitter struggle for power between the rival emperors and their legions in 69, the frequent famines and plagues that ravaged the Empire in the second half of the first century A.D.? Given the topical reference of so much of this book, this is more than likely. In that case, he is asking his readers to interpret the signs of the times correctly, and to see them as an assurance that the yearned-for coming of Christ is within sight.

> 6 ⁹When he opened the fifth seal, I saw under the altar the souls of those who had been slain for the word of God and for the witness they had borne; ¹⁰they cried out with a loud voice, 'O Sovereign

* It is possible that the words are a sardonic comment on Domitian's failure in A.D. 92 to follow through his plan to plough up vineyards for more agriculture. Popular opinion refused to harm oil and wine, and the Empire continued to enjoy a superfluity of luxuries while it went short of essentials.

† See Zech. 1⁷⁻¹⁷ and 6¹⁻⁸.

‡ Mark 13⁷⁻⁸. Luke adds 'and pestilences'. Whatever the immediate reference of this discourse (Luke makes it abundantly clear that he interprets it of the fall of Jerusalem forty years later), the signs it speaks of would obviously be taken ever afterwards as symbolic of the final coming of Christ.

Lord, holy and true, how long before thou wilt judge and avenge our blood on those who dwell upon the earth?' [11]Then they were each given a white robe and told to rest a little longer, until the number of their fellow servants and their brethren should be complete, who were to be killed as they themselves had been.

Christ has mentioned this in his discourse too:

You will stand before governors and kings for my sake, to bear testimony before them. . . . Brother will deliver up brother to death, and the father his child, and children will rise against parents and have them put to death; and you will be hated by all for my name's sake.*

Persecution and martyrdom are another sign of Christ's coming in glory: how else should his followers share that glory except by first sharing in his sacrifice?† Those who have done so have already won their victory: this is the meaning of their white robes. Nevertheless it is still possible for them to raise the agonizing cry 'How long, O Lord?' According to the first four signs, the End is imminent. What is delaying it? There would be particular point in the question when this page was first being written. The Christians who had died under Nero's persecution in the 60s of the first century might well have wondered why the End did not come there and then, in accordance with Christ's promise. John, writing during the pogrom unleashed by Domitian in the 90s, is forced to conclude that the present persecution is only the second half of the first one, and that the End cannot be far distant now. The reader must stand firm in that conviction,‡ in the knowledge that any delay can only work for the increase of God's glory, since the present world is only a machine for making God's.

6 [12]When he opened the sixth seal, I looked, and behold, there was a great earthquake; and the sun became black as sackcloth, the full moon became like blood, [13]and the stars of the sky fell to the earth as the fig tree sheds its winter fruit when shaken by a gale; [14]the sky

---

* Mark 13[9–13].

† The reference to the altar is a clear indication that martyrdom was seen as an act of sacrifice.

‡ 'A little longer' is the common burden of all apocalyptic writings.

vanished like a scroll that is rolled up, and every mountain and island was removed from its place. [15]Then the kings of the earth and the great men and the generals and the rich and the strong, and every one, slave and free, hid in the caves and among the rocks of the mountains, [16]calling to the mountains and rocks, 'Fall on us and hide us from the face of him who is seated on the throne, and from the wrath of the Lamb; [17]for the great day of their wrath has come, and who can stand before it?'

This also, for all its strange language, had formed part of Christ's discourse:

There will be earthquakes in various places. . . . The sun will be darkened, and the moon will not give its light, and the stars will be falling from heaven, and the powers in the heavens will be shaken. And then they will see the Son of Man coming in clouds with great power and glory. And then he will send out the angels, and gather his elect from the four winds, from the ends of the earth to the ends of heaven. From the fig tree learn its lesson. . . . When you see these things taking place, you know that he is near, at the very gates.*

The language is symbolic, and is not to be taken literally. God's intervention in history had always been described in such cosmic terms, particularly when this 'visitation' involved the end of an era and the beginning of a new order. Indeed, how else can such an event in the spiritual order be described except in the most spectacular terms borrowed from the material world? So Hosea and Isaiah had used exactly the same 'language of crisis' of the Assyrian invasion and the fall of Edom in the eighth century B.C., Nahum of the fall of Nineveh in the seventh century, Jeremiah of the Babylonian invasion and the deutero-Isaiah of the fall of Babylon and the return of the exiles in the sixth century, even St Peter of the coming of the Holy Spirit in the first century A.D.† It is in this context that John's words must be understood. If he speaks of the whole of mankind

---

* Mark 13[8, 24—30].

† See Hos. 10[8], Isa. 2[19], 34[4], Nah. 1[4—5], Jer. 4[24], Isa. 13[13], 50[3], Acts 2[19—20]. The hyperbolical language had become such a convention by the middle ages that the death of a rabbi in the twelfth century A.D. could be described in terms of the heavens in sackcloth, the stars in mourning, the mountains shaken, and the whole of Israel in dismay.

aghast at the upheaval of all nature,* it is to convey something
of the 'worldshaking' character of the final coming of the
Kingdom of God.

So the stage is all set for the seventh seal to be opened. The
description of the first six, each with its implicit promise that
the End is imminent, has left the reader eager to learn how the
series will be completed. But he is not to be told yet: another
whole chapter of symbolism has to be analysed before he will
have his curiosity satisfied. This withholding of the climax—
which is clearly intentional, since it is repeated in the other
series of sevens—is partly a dramatic device: it allows the tension
to be built up still more. But in this case it also has a practical
purpose: in the teeth of the kind of catastrophes which have been
promised in the first six seals, the reader needs an assurance,
such as Christ himself found it necessary to give in the discourse
quoted above, that the elect will be gathered 'from the four
winds' and spared. It is just such an assurance that is given in
this chapter:

7 ¹After this I saw four angels standing at the four corners of the
earth, holding back the four winds of the earth, that no wind might
blow on earth or sea or against any tree. ²Then I saw another angel
ascend from the rising of the sun, with the seal of the living God,
and he called with a loud voice to the four angels who had been
given power to harm earth and sea, ³saying, 'Do not harm the earth
or the sea or the trees, till we have sealed the servants of our God
upon their foreheads.' ⁴And I heard the number of the sealed, a
hundred and forty-four thousand sealed, out of every tribe of the
sons of Israel,
⁵twelve thousand sealed out of the tribe of Judah,
twelve thousand of the tribe of Reuben,
twelve thousand of the tribe of Gad,
⁶twelve thousand of the tribe of Asher,
twelve thousand of the tribe of Naphtali,
twelve thousand of the tribe of Manasseh,
⁷twelve thousand of the tribe of Simeon,
twelve thousand of the tribe of Levi,
twelve thousand of the tribe of Issachar,

---

* The listing of seven parts of nature (earth, sun, moon, stars, sky,
mountains and islands) and of seven categories of men (kings, great men,
generals, rich, strong, slave and free) is again meant to signify totality.

⁸twelve thousand of the tribe of Zebulun,
twelve thousand of the tribe of Joseph,
twelve thousand sealed out of the tribe of Benjamin.

⁹After this I looked, and behold, a great multitude which no man could number, from every nation, from all tribes and peoples and tongues, standing before the throne and before the Lamb, clothed in white robes, with palm branches in their hands, ¹⁰and crying out with a loud voice, 'Salvation belongs to our God who sits upon the throne, and to the Lamb!' ¹¹And all the angels stood round the throne and round the elders and the four living creatures, and they fell on their faces before the throne and worshipped God, ¹²saying, 'Amen! Blessing and glory wisdom and thanksgiving and honour and power and might be to our God for ever and ever! Amen.'

¹³Then one of the elders addressed me, saying, 'Who are these, clothed in white robes, and whence have they come?' ¹⁴I said to him, 'Sir, you know.' And he said to me, 'These are they who have come out the great tribulation; they have washed their robes and made them white in the blood of the Lamb.

¹⁵Therefore are they before the throne of God,
and serve him day and night within his temple;
and he who sits upon the throne
will shelter them with his presence.
¹⁶They shall hunger no more, neither thirst any more;
the sun shall not strike them, nor any scorching heat.
¹⁷For the Lamb in the midst of the throne will be their shepherd,
and he will guide them to springs of living water;
and God will wipe away every tear from their eyes.'

John has here combined Christ's promise that the elect will be spared with Ezekiel's picture of the saving of the faithful few from the punishment which God threatened to bring on sixth century Jerusalem.* It is interesting that, unlike Ezekiel, he does not say that the elect will be protected from the calamities to which Christ's coming must subject the world. It is in the midst of the war, famine, plague, persecution, martyrdom and upheaval of nature that have been described, that they are marked off as God's property, not before they have begun. John promises that they will not succumb to these catastrophes, but he cannot promise that they will be exempt from them. We shall see later the bearing this has on the concept of the Christian life taught in this book.

* Ezek. 9¹⁻¹¹.

Ezekiel had pictured his elect as being signed on the forehead with an X, as a simple mark of identification.* In reproducing this picture, does John see this X as the Cross with which Christians had identified themselves? It is more likely that he is thinking of baptism. He calls the identifying mark a 'seal' or distinctive stamp to mark Christians off from other men, and it is by this name that baptism was known from a very early age. The seal, therefore, although it is a symbol, stands for something real enough. But the numbers mentioned are pure symbolism. A thousand is simply a symbol for an immense number. A hundred and forty-four is simply the number twelve, squared to give a sense of completeness. And twelve is simply the number of the tribes of Israel, explicitly listed to drive the point home.† But these tribes too are symbolic. The passage is concerned not with the saving of the Jews as such, but with the saving of the whole Christian Church, the New Israel as it is called so frequently. In short, John's message is that the Church, the community which God has marked out as his own, in all its completeness and immensity, cannot expect to remain immune from the horrors which the coming of Christ necessarily brings in its train. But it must expect to survive them.

Parallel with the 'hundred and forty-four thousand' are the countless numbers of every nationality and language whose

* Literally, the Hebrew letter 'tau', which in Ezekiel's time was written like an X.

† All commentators note the fact that the twelve tribes are in danger of numbering thirteen. They will number twelve only if *either* Joseph *or* one of his sub-tribes Ephraim and Manasseh are included, not both. Here, curiously, *both* Joseph and Manasseh are listed. The number twelve has been maintained by leaving out one of the other tribes. Why has Dan been dropped? The tradition that the antichrist was to come from the tribe of Dan is often mentioned in this context, but since the tradition probably arose from this text it can scarcely be used as an explanation of it. More probably we are dealing with a piece of textual corruption. As the text stands, the tribes are in no order whatever, logical or chronological. By transposing the second two pairs of names (Gad, Asher, Naphtali and Manasseh) to the end of the list, an order of seniority emerges which may have been the original order (see Gen. 29-30). In this restored order, Manasseh stands precisely where one would expect to read the name Dan. Did some early copyist mistake this original word 'Dan' and write the abbreviation 'Man.' in its place?

victory is won and who sing the praises of God in heaven. Who
are these? Obviously not a group of Gentile Christians as
distinct from Jewish Christians: both have already been mingled
indistinguishably in the first group of the New Israel. This
second group must be seen either as the Christians already in
heaven, whose company the New Israel on earth have been
marked out eventually to join, or perhaps even as the *same*
group, previously marked out for salvation in the midst of their
sufferings, now offering their thanksgiving to God in heaven.
Nor is it any objection to such an interpretation that the same
group cannot at one moment be specified as a hundred and
forty-four thousand, and the next called 'countless.' In apocalyptic language, a hundred and forty-four thousand *is* countless.

In either case, the final verses indicate that we have reached a
climax. When hunger and thirst and mourning are banished,
when all misfortune is done away with and all desire satisfied,
there is little more that can be added. By a sublime paradox,
John pictures the Lamb now become a shepherd, leading those
who have washed their robes white in his red blood to the object
of all their yearning, the intimate presence of God. The Greek
word used for this presence has the same letters as 'Shekinah',
the Hebrew word used of that intimacy with God which was
once thought to have characterized the Jerusalem temple, and
whose return the later books of the Old Testament all long for
as the end of all things.* John says that in this vision that
longed-for reality has been achieved.†

With that assurance given, then, that the elect will survive all
the cataclysms so far described, the reader is finally ready to
hear about the last of the seven seals. If the giving of that
assurance has interrupted the regular rhythm set by the opening
of the first six seals, and delayed the final revelation until now,
he should be all the more impatient to find out what happens

---

* See Hag. 2⁷, Zech. 2 ⁵,¹⁰, Song. 8¹⁴, Isa. 64¹, Mal. 3¹.

† Exactly the same play on words is used in the Fourth Gospel, where
the well-known phrase 'he dwelt amongst us' (1¹⁴) really means 'the Shekinah
dwelt in our midst.'

when the last of the seals is broken, and the scroll can at last be
unrolled.

8 [1]When the Lamb opened the seventh seal, there was silence in
heaven for about half an hour.

If that is the end of the series of seven seals—and the fact that
the next verse begins on another series of sevens would suggest
that it is—then we have here what is perhaps the most overwhelming revelation of the whole book. This is, finally, the
climax, the end, the consummation, and it is unspeakable,
inexpressible, something 'which no apocalypse can reveal.*
However, it is equally possible that the next verse has been
misplaced, and that the solemn silence here enjoined is to allow
what follows to be heard:

8 [1]When the Lamb opened the seventh seal, there was silence in
heaven for about half an hour. [3]And an(other) angel came and stood
at the altar with a golden censer; and he was given much incense
to mingle with the prayers of all the saints upon the golden altar
before the throne; [4]and the smoke of the incense rose with the
prayers of the saints from the hand of the angel before God. [5]Then
the angel took the censer and filled it with fire from the altar and
threw it on the earth; and there were peals of thunder, loud noises,
flashes of lightning, and an earthquake.

In this case, the silence which reigns in heaven is simply to
allow the prayer of the martyrs on earth—5[8] has identified the
incense with their prayer and 6[10] has given us an example of
their cry—to be heard. And heard it is. In answer to their
agonized pleading, the divine thunderbolt is despatched from
heaven to destroy their persecutors, and thunder and earthquake
and lightning announce, as always, the fact that God has finally
come.†

In either case, whether it is a question of the ineffable
consummation or of the final coming of God, no doubt can be
left in the reader's mind that he has reached the End. The
analysis of the first six seals have already contained that

---

* Martindale, *op. cit.* p. 66.　　　† See the comment on 4[5].

message implicitly. The seventh simply makes it explicit. This is the totality of the revelation that John has to offer the reader, even though he is going to make several more attempts to present it to him again. Its meaning should now be clear: Christ's eschatological discourse had already set the pattern, with wars, famines, plagues, persecution, cosmic disturbances and the sparing of the elect all preceding the 'End', his own coming. If John has used the same sequence of events, it is because he reckons that many of them have already taken place in the wars, famines and plagues of the 60s, perhaps most especially in the martyrdoms of the 60s, which every Christian at the time must have regarded as the definitive sign that the End was imminent. John, writing in the 90s, can only assure his readers that the new martyrdoms in some way complete the old ones, and that the End cannot be far distant now. With the object of their yearning so nearly within sight and so closely within their grasp, will they not endure a little longer?

2. The Seven Trumpets

The series begins again at the beginning, with the presumption that we know nothing yet. The seven trumpets are not a sequel to the seven seals, as if they were sounded after the half-hour's silence of 8^1. They form a complete and independent series on their own, comprising again the totality of the revelation which John has to give to us. They are another recapitulation of his theme, constructed along exactly the same lines as the first seven.

8 ^{2}Then I saw the seven angels who stand before God, and seven trumpets were given to them. ^{6}Now the seven angels who had the seven trumpets made ready to blow them.

^{7}The first angel blew his trumpet, and there followed hail and fire, mixed with blood, which fell on the earth; and a third of the earth was burnt up, and a third of the trees were burnt up, and all green grass was burnt up.

^{8}The second angel blew his trumpet, and something like a great mountain, burning with fire, was thrown into the sea; ^{9}and a third of the sea became blood, a third of the living creatures in the sea died, and a third of the ships were destroyed.

¹⁰The third angel blew his trumpet, and a great star fell from heaven, blazing like a torch, and it fell on a third of the rivers and on the fountains of water. ¹¹The name of the star is Wormwood. A third of the waters became wormwood, and many men died of the water, because it was made bitter.

¹²The fourth angel blew his trumpet, and a third of the sun was struck, and a third of the moon, and a third of the stars, so that a third of their light was darkened; a third of the day was kept from shining, and likewise a third of the night.

For this first quartet, John has gone to the book of Exodus. The very notion of a trumpet blast as an announcement of God's presence is borrowed from the theophany at mount Sinai, a theophany which had a profound influence on all subsequent descriptions of the coming of God.* This alone would make it unnecessary to look for any specific reality corresponding to the drought, disease, death and destruction which are here described as ravaging the land, the sea, the rivers and the sky. Given the fact that the Exodus story is being used as a prototype of the way in which God acts on behalf of his people, one would expect its details to provide John with the imagery in which to describe the intervention of God that he is concerned with. The four trumpet blasts are in fact simply an echo of the plagues which tradition connected with the Israelite escape from Egypt,† symbols of the punishment which God inflicts on those who resist him when he comes to save his people. It is again probable however that they are not mere symbols, but are meant to remind the reader of events he has already witnessed—hailstorms, eclipses, perhaps especially the eruption of Vesuvius in the year 79—which John is asking him to see as signs that the End is at hand.

Awe-inspiring as the apocalyptic description of these events is, it pales into insignificance in the light of what is to follow.

---

* Ps. 47⁵, Isa. 27¹³, Joel 2¹, ¹⁵, Zeph. 1¹⁶, Zech. 9¹⁴, Matt. 24³¹, 1 Cor. 15² and 1 Thess. 4¹⁶ all depend on Exod. 19¹³⁻¹⁸.

† The hail corresponds with the seventh plague (Exod. 9²⁴⁻²⁷), the destruction of sea-life and river-life with the first (Exod. 7²⁰⁻²¹), and the darkening of the sun with the ninth (Exod. 10²²⁻²³).

The fifth trumpet blast is accordingly introduced by a solemn announcement of the 'woes' still to come:*

8 ¹³Then I looked, and I heard an eagle crying with a loud voice, as it flew in midheaven, 'Woe, woe, woe to those who dwell on the earth, at the blasts of the other trumpets which the three angels are about to blow!'
9 ¹And the fifth angel blew his trumpet, and I saw a star fallen from heaven to earth, and he was given the key of the shaft of the bottomless pit; ²he opened the shaft of the bottomless pit, and from the shaft rose smoke like the smoke of a great furnace, and the sun and the air were darkened with the smoke from the shaft. ³Then from the smoke came locusts on the earth, and they were given power like the power of the scorpions of the earth; ⁴they were told not to harm the grass of the earth or any green growth or any tree, but only those of mankind who have not the seal of God upon their foreheads; ⁵they were allowed to torture them for five months, but not to kill them, and their torture was like the torture of a scorpion, when it stings a man. ⁶And in those days men will seek death and will not find it; they will long to die, and death flies from them.
⁷In appearance the locusts were like horses arrayed for battle; on their heads were what looked like crowns of gold; their faces were like human faces, ⁸their hair like women's hair, and their teeth like lions' teeth; ⁹they had scales like iron breastplates, and the noise of their wings was like the noise of many chariots with horses rushing into battle; ¹⁰they have tails like scorpions, and stings, and their power of hurting men for five months lies in their tails. ¹¹They have as king over them the angel of the bottomless pit; his name in Hebrew is Abaddon, and in Greek he is called Apollyon.
¹²The first woe has passed; behold, two woes are still to come.

A number of different elements have gone to make up this phantasmagoria. The primary source, as for the pictures called forth by the first four trumpets,† is again the book of Exodus, where an invasion of locusts—with their life span of five months, generally from April to August—is included among the ten

---

* This device, like the delaying tactic inserted between the sixth and the seventh of these series of seven, is presumably used to heighten the reader's curiosity about what is to follow. 9¹² and 11¹⁴ will inform us that the fifth and sixth trumpets comprise the first two woes. The third is left unspecified, although both the casting down of Satan to the earth in 12¹² and the fall of Babylon in 18¹⁰, ¹⁶, ¹⁹ are marked by the same Greek word for 'woe'.

† With which this picture is not entirely consistent: the grass which is here ordered to be spared should, according to 8⁷, already have been destroyed.

plagues. Basically, therefore, we are still dealing with the traditional imagery in which the saving intervention of God was described.

But John has also gone to the book of Joel, with its brilliant presentation of a plague of locusts as if it were a mailed army on the move:

> A day of darkness and gloom,
> a day of clouds and thick darkness!
> Like blackness there is spread upon the mountains
> a great and powerful people . . .
> Their appearance is like the appearance of horses,
> and like war horses they run.
> As with the rumbling of chariots,
> they leap on the tops of the mountains . . .
> like a powerful army drawn up for battle . . .
> Its teeth are lions' teeth,
> and it has the fangs of a lioness.*

Superimposed upon this picture of a plague of locusts is another, of a plague of scorpions, which strike at men not indirectly by ravaging their food, but directly by inflicting a sting which can cause the most acute suffering.

The final concept superimposed on this already complex picture is that of an invasion of Parthian horsemen, with their characteristically long and flowing hair. The physical appearance of locusts, with their horny bodies, and heads not unlike those of horses,† had already made it possible to describe an armoured cavalry in these terms, and the tail-sting of scorpions provided a link with the sharpshooting Parthians, who were notorious for firing arrows over the back of their shoulder.

It is this last 'layer', as it were, of the composite picture which is the most prominent in John's mind. As he had already suggested in 6^2, the Parthian army, massed on the eastern border of the Empire, constituted a permanent threat to Rome's safety. It had already marched once in the year 62, and there

---

* Joel. 2^{2-5}, 1^6.
† The colloquial Italian and German words for locust are *cavalletta* and *Heupferd*, literally 'little horse' and 'hay-horse'.

was a recurrent rumour that when Nero was reputed to have committed suicide in 68, he had really fled East, whence he would return at the head of a Parthian army to take vengeance on the Rome that had rejected him. As this prospect grew less and less likely with the years, the return of Nero was expected from the underworld, at the head of a demonic army. Both rumours are reflected in this vision of the Parthian scourge, arising from the 'bottomless pit'* and led by a king named 'Destruction'. It is a message of doom for Rome, and therefore one of hope for the Christian bowed down under Rome's yoke. The reader is being assured again, as he was in 7^{1-8}, that this scourge has no power to harm—permanently—those who are marked with God's seal.

The sixth trumpet blast is nothing more than a further development of the fifth:

9 ^{13}Then the sixth angel blew his trumpet, and I heard a voice from the four horns of the golden altar before God, ^{14}saying to the sixth angel who had the trumpet, 'Release the four angels who are bound at the great river Euphrates.' ^{15}So the four angels were released, who had been held ready for the hour, the day, the month, and the year, to kill a third of mankind.

^{16}The number of the troops of cavalry was twice ten thousand times ten thousand; I heard their number. ^{17}And this was how I saw the horses in my vision: the riders wore breastplates the colour of fire and of sapphire and of sulphur, and the heads of the horses were like lions' heads, and fire and smoke and sulphur issued from their mouths. ^{18}By these three plagues a third of mankind was killed, by the fire and smoke and sulphur issuing from their mouths. ^{19}For the power of the horses is in their mouths and in their tails; their tails are like serpents, with heads, and by means of them they wound.

^{20}The rest of mankind, who were not killed by these plagues, did not repent of the works of their hands nor give up worshipping demons and idols of gold and silver and bronze and stone and wood, which cannot either see or hear or walk; ^{21}nor did they repent of their murders or their sorceries or their immorality or their thefts

---

* The mysterious subterranean region inhabited by the dead and the elements hostile to God. It will recur again in 11^7, 17^8 and 20^1. The falling star that opens it in 9^1 has no bearing on the concept of fallen angels. The phrase is exactly parallel to the one used in 20^1.

The Euphrates is mentioned precisely as the eastern border of the Roman empire, behind which lay poised the threat which haunted Roman minds, the Parthian cavalry. The reference to the 'sting in the tail' links the scene with the previous reference to their sharpshooting. With its nightmarish colours and its chimerical numbers, the imagery is in some ways even more fantastic than before. But for the readers John has in mind, schooled in the 'dialect' of apocalyptic language, there would be no difficulty in translating the symbols into the one concept they were meant to evoke. They would see the Parthian invasion, as John wishes them to see it, as the answer to the pleading of persecuted Christians, whose prayers were represented in 8^3 as being offered at the golden altar with which the vision begins. Not that this makes the Parthians a salutary force: the four angels which are said to lead them stem from a mentality which attributed guardian angels to all things, beneficial or baneful.* But the prospect of this eastern peril invading the Roman empire—a very real prospect at the time of writing—formed for John another of the signs that 'the hour, the day, the month, the year' is at hand. The same conviction had been expressed in reference to the sixth of the first series of seven.†

The stage is therefore once more set for the climax, which the piecemeal analysis of the first six visions in this series of seven has led the reader to expect. But once more he is baulked of his expectation—this time for even longer than in the first series—so that the tension can again be heightened, and the assurance given that in the midst of these apocalyptic disasters the elect will be spared:

10 [1]Then I saw another mighty angel coming down from heaven, wrapped in a cloud, with a rainbow over his head, and his face was like the sun, and his legs like pillars of fire. [2]He had a little scroll open in his hand. And he set his right foot on the sea, and his left foot on the land, [3]and called out with a loud voice, like a lion roaring; when he called out, the seven thunders sounded. [4]And

* See on 1^{20} above. † See 6^{16}.

when the seven thunders had sounded, I was about to write, but I heard a voice from heaven saying, 'Seal up what the seven thunders have said, and do not write it down.' [5]And the angel whom I saw standing on sea and land lifted up his right hand to heaven [6]and swore by him who lives for ever and ever, who created heaven and what is in it, and the sea and what is in it, that there should be no more delay, [7]but that in the day of the trumpet call to be sounded by the seventh angel, the mystery of God, as he announced to his servants the prophets, should be fulfilled.

[8]Then the voice which I had heard from heaven spoke to me again, saying, 'Go, take the scroll which is open in the hand of the angel who is standing on the sea and on the land.' [9]So I went to the angel and told him to give me the little scroll; and he said to me, 'Take it and eat; it will be bitter to your stomach, but sweet as honey in your mouth.' [10]And I took the little scroll from the hand of the angel and ate it; it was sweet as honey in my mouth, but when I had eaten it my stomach was made bitter. [11]And I was told, 'You must again prophesy about many peoples and nations and tongues and kings.'

The digression from the main theme concerns the scroll whose contents will be described in ch. 11. It is introduced by an angel whose description outshines, in sheer awe-inspiring magnificence, that of any other in this angel-studded book.* This itself may distract us into asking the meaning of the enigmatic seven thunders which echo to the sound of his voice, and the reason for the solemn oath that he swears that there will be no further interruptions.† But both details seem to be no more than added dramatic devices to ensure that the reader's interest is kept at fever-pitch. Both are meant to convince him that, whatever mysteries still remain unresolved for him now, he will before the end of ch. 11 (again) be in possession of the full explanation of God's plan. His interest, meanwhile, is focused on the scroll.

Unlike the scroll of ch. 5 whose seven seals provided the material of the first series of seven, this one is unsealed. In other words, its contents are not, as in the previous scroll, a divine mystery which it requires the death and resurrection of Christ

---

* Not that even this brilliant description is entirely original. It depends very largely on Dan. 10[5-6] and 12[5-7].

† The Douay's 'no more time', dependent on the Latin, is a mistranslation of the Greek original.

to elucidate. They are an open secret, which all the readers may be expected to recognise immediately. This is not to say that they can easily be described. John himself, when he makes them his own,* finds them ambiguously sweet and bitter at the same time: presumably they speak of both triumph and suffering. What is this paradox? John's outline of it is as complex as anything he has yet attempted to describe:

11 ¹Then I was given a measuring rod like a staff, and I was told: 'Rise and measure the temple of God and the altar and those who worship there, ²but do not measure the court outside the temple; leave that out, for it is given over to the nations, and they will trample over the holy city for forty-two months. ³And I will grant my two witnesses power to prophesy for one thousand two hundred and sixty days, clothed in sack-cloth.

⁴These are the two olive trees and the two lampstands which stand before the Lord of the earth. ⁵And if anyone would harm them, fire pours from their mouth and consumes their foes; if anyone would harm them, thus he is doomed to be killed. ⁶They have power to shut the sky, that no rain may fall during the days of their prophesying, and they have power over the waters to turn them into blood, and to smite the earth with every plague, as often as they desire. ⁷And when they have finished their testimony, the beast that ascends from the bottomless pit will make war upon them and conquer them and kill them, ⁸and their dead bodies will lie in the street of the great city which is allegorically called Sodom and Egypt, where their Lord was crucified. ⁹For three days and a half men from the peoples and tribes and tongues and nations gaze at their dead bodies and refuse to let them be placed in a tomb, ¹⁰and those who dwell on the earth will rejoice over them and make merry and exchange presents, because these two prophets had been a torment to those who dwell on the earth. ¹¹But after the three and a half days a breath of life from God entered them, and they stood up on their feet, and great fear fell on those who saw them. ¹²Then they heard a loud voice from heaven saying to them, 'Come up hither!' And in the sight of their foes they went up to heaven in a cloud. ¹³And at that hour there was a great earthquake, and a tenth of the city fell; seven thousand people were killed in the earthquake, and the rest were terrified and gave glory to the God of heaven.

¹⁴The second woe has passed; behold, the third woe is soon to come.

---

* The symbolism of 'eating' a scroll in order to master its contents is borrowed from Ezek. 2⁹-3³.

The place where this scene is set—the 'Holy City', the great
city where the 'Lord was crucified'—is clearly Jerusalem.* If
it is also called 'Sodom and Egypt', this is explicitly an allegorical
comment on its rejection of the revelation which God had made
to it in the person of Christ. For this, it is 'given over to the
nations' to be trampled under. The fact that the 'beast from the
bottomless pit' is involved in this disaster suggests that these
nations are to be identified with the power of Rome, for that is
the meaning of the beast already suggested in 9^{11} and to be made
explicit in ch. 13. The time in which this event takes place,
according to the opening verses at least, is boldly set in the
future—a common enough feature in apocalyptic literature. But
the scene finishes lamely in the past tense, as if John was not
able to keep up the pretence; he is really describing something
that has already taken place.

Basically, therefore, we are dealing with the Roman siege of
Jerusalem in the year 70. This is the message contained in the
'open scroll', readily recognized by the book's first readers, who
had become used to seeing the destruction of Jerusalem at the
end of the Jewish War as a divine judgment on a nation which
had rejected Christ. In actual historical fact, this 'trampling
under' of Jerusalem took the Roman armies only a few weeks.
If John speaks of a period of 1260 days (or forty two months, or
three and a half years—the periods are meant to be equivalent),
this must be understood symbolically, for since Maccabean
times, when Antiochus IV's attempt to obliterate Jewish
religion had lasted for exactly this amount of time,† the period
had become a stereotype, and was used to designate 'persecution
time', whether this was in reality long or short. Since the

---

* Some commentators, taking the two martyred witnesses to be Peter and
Paul, suggest that the reference to the crucifixion is a gloss and understand
the scene to be set in Rome, which is regularly called 'the Great City' in
ch. 16, 17 and 18. But the Apocalypse shows no interest in Rome itself, as a
town, and as will be shown below, the two witnesses are better understood
symbolically rather than as two specific persons.

† From June 168 to December 165 B.C. See 1 Macc. 1^{20}ff. and Dan. 7^{25},
8^{14}, 9^{27} and 12^{7}, where the period is sometimes called (as here in 12^{14}) 'a time
(i.e. a year) and (two) times and half a time.'

number three and a half is also the half of seven, it suggests totality split into two and therefore incomplete. It is a period which is essentially limited, which cannot last.*

However, the purpose of this interlude is not simply to recall the siege of Jerusalem. The scene is described to record the sparing of the 'temple and those who worshipped there', for that is the symbolism of the measuring rod.† Under the figure of the temple, John has in mind the Christian community in Jerusalem during the late sixties of the first century. Warned by Christ's prediction of the city's destruction, they had fled well before the Roman onslaught reached its climax, and had been spared the slaughter that ensued. But not all of them were able to escape. Under the figure of the two witnesses John remembers those who remained behind during this 'persecution time' and continued to bear witness to the Christian message. Their martyrdom finally seemed to silence them and to mark their ultimate failure. But this triumph of godlessness was shortlived. John assures the reader that, like the Christ they served, they were accorded a resurrection after three days and an ascension to their reward in heaven.‡ The city's destruction, described in typical 'apocalyptic' imagery, was God's visible vindication of their witness.

For this picture of Christian witness in the last days of Jerusalem, John has made use of descriptions which already existed. The two well-known pairs—Moses and Elijah, Joshua and Zerubbabel§—form as it were the pattern on which

---

* Under the form of 'forty-two months' the period may be meant to suggest the totally (seven) incomplete thing (six).

† The symbolism is again taken from the book of Ezekiel, where a whole section (ch. 40-44) is devoted to a detailed and measured plan of the future messianic community in terms of an ideal temple. Jerusalem is also measured in Zechariah 2^{5-9} as a symbol of its restoration and protection by God.

‡ The number three and a half is again being used to denote a period of time which is fatally limited, infinitely more so even than the persecution time of three and a half years.

§ V. 4 is a direct quotation of Zechariah 4^3 and 4^{14}. Vv. 5-6 recall the plagues Moses called down upon Egypt (Exod. 7^{17}, 11^{10}), and the drought by which Elijah drove home his message 1 Ki. 17^1. V. 12 refers to the fact that not only Elijah (2 Ki. 2^{11}) but, according to Jewish legend, Moses as well (*The Assumption of Moses*) was taken up into heaven.

Christians must base their task of bearing witness to the God of Sinai and building up the messianic community. This seems to be the only reason why the witnesses are described as 'two', and no purpose is served in searching for a Christian pair to correspond to them. They stand for all the Jerusalem Christians who bore witness to their faith in this first clash between the Church and the might of Rome. Their example must be followed by all Christians, who must remain convinced that in the inner sanctuary of their hearts they will remain unharmed, even though they are doomed to persecution, death and apparent failure in the 'court outside'. These are necessarily two complementary aspects of the Kingdom, the message that is both sweet and bitter at the same time. The long digression has served basically the same purpose as the message which interrupted the first series of seven.

So the scene is once more set for the finale, the seventh tableau for which the first six, and even more the digression, have aroused all the reader's curiosity:

> **11** [15]Then the seventh angel blew his trumpet, and there were loud voices in heaven, saying, 'The kingdom of the world has become the kingdom of our Lord and of his Christ, and he shall reign for ever and ever.' [16]And the twenty-four elders who sit on their thrones before God fell on their faces and worshipped God, [17]saying,
> 'We give thanks to thee, Lord God almighty, who art and who wast, that thou hast taken thy great power and begun to reign.
> [18]The nations raged, but thy wrath came,
> and the time for the dead to be judged,
> for rewarding thy servants, the prophets and saints,
> and those who fear thy name, both small and great,
> and for destroying the destroyers of the earth.'

To that, nothing more can be added. When God's Kingdom has been achieved, the end has come. The song of the twenty-four marks the finality of the scene. If God had previously been described as the one 'who is and who was and who is to come',* he is here simply 'who art and who wast'. The last part of the

---

* See 1[4,8], 4[8].

original title no longer applies. His future coming is now present. The final consummation has taken place.

The message of the seven trumpets is exactly parallel to the one already expressed under the figure of the seven seals. The same cosmic symbolism has been pressed into service in order to lead to the same climax. John has directed his readers' attention to events which both he and they had already experienced—the eclipses and hailstorms of the first century, the Parthian attack of 62, the fall of Jerusalem in 70, the eruption of Vesuvius in 79. If he has spoken of these in the future tense, it is only because he is using the apocalyptic idiom and showing that past history is linked with the future in one chain of events. The reader must see those six events of the past as a guarantee of the seventh, which is the final victory of the establishment of God's Kingdom.

3. The Seven Bowls of Wrath

The last of these series of seven is based so closely on the one we have just considered that it is impossible to regard it as a sequel to it. It is simply another repetition of it, under a slightly different formula.* This is emphasised by its very opening words, which insist that the seven ensuing plagues are the last. Any further ones which may be described later in the book—and there are plenty—must not be regarded as a sequel to these, which are to be interpreted as another attempt to describe the complete plan of God.†

> **15** ¹Then I saw another portent in heaven, great and wonderful, seven angels with seven plagues, which are the last, for with them the wrath of God is ended.

* For this reason it will be more convenient to deal with it here, and to leave the discussion of the intervening chapters 12-14 until later.

† As was the case with 8², it would seem that the opening verse of this vision has been misplaced—perhaps deliberately in order to interlock the various sections of which the book is made up. This has obscured the fact that 15²⁻⁴ probably belongs to the vision of ch. 12-14 (in the same way that 8³⁻⁵, it was suggested above, probably belongs to the vision of ch. 6-7). The verses will be dealt with in the appropriate section below.

⁵(After this) I looked, and the temple of the tent of witness in heaven was opened, ⁶and out of the temple came the seven angels with the seven plagues, robed in pure white linen, and their breasts girded with golden girdles. ⁷And one of the four living creatures gave the seven angels seven golden bowls full of the wrath of God who lives for ever and ever; ⁸and the temple was filled with smoke from the glory of God and from his power, and no one could enter the temple until the seven plagues of the seven angels were ended.

16 ¹Then I heard a loud voice from the temple telling the seven angels, 'Go and pour out on the earth the seven bowls of the wrath of God.'

²So the first angel went and poured his bowl on the earth, and foul and evil sores came upon the men who bore the mark of the beast and worshipped its image.

³The second angel poured his bowl into the sea, and it became like the blood of a dead man, and every living thing died that was in the sea.

⁴The third angel poured his bowl into the rivers and the fountains of water, and they became blood. ⁵And I heard the angel of water say,

'Just art thou in these thy judgments,
thou who art and wast, O Holy One.
⁶For men have shed the blood of saints and prophets,
and thou hast given them blood to drink.
It is their due!'

⁷And I heard the altar cry,

'Yea, Lord God the Almighty,
true and just are thy judgments!'

⁸The fourth angel poured his bowl on the sun, and it was allowed to scorch men with fire; ⁹men were scorched by the fierce heat, and they cursed the name of God who had power over these plagues, and they did not repent and give him glory.

The opening of the heavens is a technique that was used in the very first vision (4¹); the reader must be convinced that he is witnessing a divine revelation. The rest of the description is also such a conscious echo of what has gone before that there is no need to dwell long on it. Like the first quartet of trumpets, the first four bowls of wrath are described in terms of the Egyptian plagues,* and symbolize the punishment of those who resist

---

* The first bowl is reminiscent of the sixth plague in Exod. 9⁸⁻¹². The rest are as before.

God's saving intervention. The reference is therefore too generic to make it necessary to specify them, but it is probable that, as before, John has certain events of the first century in mind—epidemics, droughts and perhaps especially the eruption of Vesuvius—and again invites the reader to see in them the judgment of God, who is significantly described, as at the end of the previous vision, in his past and present eternity (v. 5), but not in his future. That has come.

16 10The fifth angel poured his bowl on the throne of the beast, and its kingdom was in darkness; men gnawed their tongues in anguish 11and cursed the God of heaven for their pain and sores, and did not repent of their deeds.

12The sixth angel poured his bowl on the great river Euphrates, and its water was dried up, to prepare the way for the kings from the east.

The Euphrates has already been mentioned in 9¹⁴ as the frontier which contained the Parthians, who in the first century constituted the biggest threat to the safety of the bestial Roman Empire.* Both these visions therefore look forward, as did 6² and 9³ᶠᶠ·, to the invasion of these eastern forces to destroy the throne on which the Church's persecutor was seated. This prospect would again lead the reader to expect the end to follow. But just as in the other series of seven, this end is delayed—though here for only a short time—to heighten the dramatic effect and to guarantee again the sparing of the elect from the cataclysms that have made up the first six visions.

16 13And I saw, issuing from the mouth of the dragon and from the mouth of the beast and from the mouth of the false prophet, three foul spirits like frogs; 14for they are demonic spirits, performing signs, who go abroad to the kings of the whole world, to assemble them for battle on the great day of God the Almighty. 15('Lo, I am coming like a thief! Blessed is he who is awake, keeping his garments that he may not go naked and be seen exposed!') 16And they assembled them at the place which is called in Hebrew Armageddon.

* That the 'Beast' refers to Rome will be clearer after the analysis of ch. 12-14, which for the sake of convenience we have left until later.

The demonic trio here introduced—the Dragon, the Beast and
the false Prophet—represent Satan, Rome and the emperor-
cult.* It is their ridiculous croakings which have attracted all the
world's nations to assemble together, ripe for God's judgment·

This judgment John places in Armageddon or the Heights of
Megiddo. Megiddo guards a narrow defile in the Carmel range,
through which all north-south traffic in Palestine must pass. It
was the scene of many decisive battles throughout Old Testament history† and so provides John with a fitting symbol for the
final conflict, on the Day of the Lord, between God and the
forces of evil. From this condemnatory judgment too, the
Christian will be spared. If he remains faithful to the righteousness with which God has clothed him, he has no need to fear
this coming of God.

The climax for which this interruption has only heightened
the interest may now be disclosed:

16 [17]The seventh angel poured his bowl into the air, and a great
voice came out of the temple, from the throne, saying, 'It is done!'

Clearly, with language like that, this is the End, and it is no
use reading the chapters which follow as a sequel to this. They
can only be interpreted as another attempt to describe the same
thing. Here it is described in terms to which we have by now
become used:

[18]And there were flashes of lightning, loud noises, peals of
thunder, and a great earthquake such as had never been since men
were on the earth, so great was that earthquake. [19]The great city

---

* See the analysis of ch. 12-14 below.

† Both the Egyptian pharaohs Thutmosis III and Ramesses II fought at
Megiddo. It is mentioned as the scene of one of Joshua's victories (Jos. 12[21]),
as well as of Barak against the Canaanites and of Gideon against the
Midianites (Judges 5 and 7). Solomon made it one of his fortifications
(1 Ki. 9[15]). The pretender to the Israelite throne Jehu made sure of his
throne there (2 Ki. 9[27]), and later Josiah lost it there to the Egyptian invader
Neco (4 Ki. 23[29]). It figures in the records of the Assyrians Shalmaneser and
Tiglath Pileser, the Greek Alexander the Great and the Roman Pompey. In
more recent times Napoleon fought there, and it was the scene of Turkey's
defeat by Lord Allenby ('Allenby of Megiddo'), an event which was the
beginning of the end of World War I.

was split into three parts, and the cities of the nations fell, and God remembered great Babylon, to make her drain the cup of the fury of his wrath. [20]And every island fled away, and no mountains were to be found; [21]and great hailstones, heavy as a hundredweight, dropped on men from heaven, till men cursed God for the plague of the hail, so fearful was that plague.

The great city of Babylon is John's cryptogram for Rome.[*] In the apocalyptic language of crisis, he describes its destruction under the punishing hand of God—as he will do several more times later. The language cannot be taken literally: only cosmic terms will serve to convey the 'earthshaking' nature of an event on which the whole series has been focused.

To conclude this already overlong section: like those which preceded it, the seven bowls of wrath comprise a series complete in itself. It contains too many references to the End to allow us to see it as part of a larger series. As before, a number of events which the reader has already witnessed are appealed to as signs that the End is upon him. They lead inevitably and inescapably, in one chain, to the destruction of the forces of evil and the final victory of God. This, the reader must now be convinced, is as good as present.

The Serpent (*chapters* 12-14)

The sevens are over. The fifth statement of the book's theme reverts to the method used in the first (The Lamb), and presents the revelation in three tableaux in sequence to each other. The technique used to introduce these is also reminiscent of that first vision, where the heavens opened as they do here to convince the reader that he is being given an insight into God's secrets. And the ark of the covenant that he there sees disclosed is to be his guarantee—as it was for the Israel of the Old Testament— that God keeps his promise. Jewish tradition had it[†] that when the temple was destroyed by the Babylonians, the

---

[*] The term is again taken from ch. 12-14, which will be dealt with below
[†] See 2 Macc. 2[5—8].

prophet Jeremiah had rescued the ark of the covenant and
hidden it until God saw fit to reveal it again in the messianic age,
as the symbol of the new and eternal covenant he would then
make with mankind. John wishes to assure his reader, before
even these new visions begin, that this messianic age has come.
The issue is predetermined, before he has even begun to
describe it.

1. The Woman

11 ¹⁹Then God's temple in heaven was opened, and the ark of his
covenant was seen within his temple; and there were flashes of
lightning, loud noises, peals of thunder, an earthquake, and heavy
hail.

12 ¹And a great portent appeared in heaven, a woman clothed
with the sun, with the moon under her feet, and on her head a
crown of twelve stars; ²and she was with child and she cried out in
her pangs of birth, in anguish for delivery. ³And another portent
appeared in heaven; behold a great red dragon, with seven heads and
ten horns, and seven diadems upon his heads. ⁴His tail swept down
a third of the stars of heaven, and cast them to the earth. And the
dragon stood before the woman who was about to bear a child, that
he might devour her child when she brought it forth; ⁵she brought
forth a male child, one who is to rule all the nations with a rod of
iron, but her child was caught up to God and to his throne, ⁶and the
woman fled into the wilderness, where she has a place prepared by
God, in which to be nourished for one thousand two hundred and
sixty days.

⁷Now war arose in heaven, Michael and his angels fighting against
the dragon; and the dragon and his angels fought, ⁸but they were
defeated and there was no longer any place for them in heaven.
⁹And the great dragon was thrown down, that ancient serpent, who
is called the Devil and Satan, the deceiver of the whole world—he
was thrown down to the earth, and his angels were thrown down
with him. ¹⁰And I heard a loud voice in heaven, saying, 'Now the
salvation and the power and the kingdom of our God and the
authority of his Christ have come, for the accuser of our brethren
has been thrown down, who accuses them day and night before our
God. ¹¹And they have conquered him by the blood of the Lamb and
by the word of their testimony, for they loved not their lives even
unto death. ¹²Rejoice then, O heaven and you that dwell therein!
But woe to you, O earth and sea, for the devil has come down to
you in great wrath, because he knows that his time is short!'

¹³And when the dragon saw that he had been thrown down to the earth, he pursued the woman who had borne the male child. ¹⁴But the woman was given the two wings of the great eagle that she might fly from the serpent into the wilderness, to the place where she is to be nourished for a time, and times, and half a time. ¹⁵The serpent poured water like a river out of his mouth after the woman, to sweep her away with the flood. ¹⁶But the earth came to the help of the woman, and the earth opened its mouth and swallowed the river which the dragon had poured from his mouth. ¹⁷Then the dragon was angry with the woman, and went off to make war on the rest of her offspring, on those who keep the commandments of God and bear testimony to Jesus. And he stood on the sand of the sea.

The vision proper, then, begins with the figure of a Woman clothed with the sun and the stars. We think naturally enough of our Lady, to whom this description has traditionally been applied. After all, we say, of whom else could John be thinking when he speaks of the mother of the Messiah?* However it is clear from the rest of the chapter that this interpretation will stand only if the verse is isolated: what follows has very little relevance to our Lady. Nor is it any honour to Mary to apply any and every text to her without thought. We are dealing here with an apocalyptic writing, which speaks in terms that are not meant to be taken literally. Outside of such literature a description of the woman who gives birth to the Messiah might well put us in mind of Bethlehem. But we are not taking photographs here; we are talking in symbols, and the birth is symbolic, and so is the Dragon, and so is the Woman.

Who then is she? The source to which John has turned for his imagery throughout this book is the Old Testament. There, *the* Woman, the bride of God who brings forth the Messiah, is Israel, the true Israel, the chosen people of God.† It is quite certain that this is what is in John's mind when he begins his description with a quotation from Gen. 37⁹⁻¹⁰, where the sun and moon and twelve stars represent the twelve-fold Israel.‡

* The words of v. 5 are taken from the messianic psalm 2.
† See Isa. 62¹⁻⁹, Mic. 4⁹-5⁴, Joel 2²³⁻²⁷, Zech. 2¹⁴, Zeph. 3¹⁴⁻¹⁸.
‡ The quotation is echoed in the Song of Solomon 6¹⁰, where the Woman clothed in light, fair as the moon and bright as the sun, is again Israel.

This Woman will later be contrasted with the Harlot (the collective personality of Rome, opposed to the true Israel),* and will be specified at the end of the book, again appearing in light and splendour for her marriage with the Lamb, as the twelve-gated Jerusalem which forms the new Israel.† In fact the number twelve occurs so frequently in the Apocalypse in reference to Israel‡ that it cannot have a different meaning here. All the early Fathers of the Church interpreted these verses as about the Israel of God.

What then is John trying to say? According to the prophets, the Messiah was to be born of the true Israel. In the event, that true Israel was reduced to a tiny group, at the centre of which stood the twelve apostles. It was in their anguish and sorrow that the crucified Jesus became the Messiah. Had he not told them so himself, in precisely this same language, shortly before he died?

'A little while, and you will not see me,
and again a little while, and you will see me.
Truly, truly, I say to you,
you will weep and lament, but the world will rejoice;
you will be sorrowful, but your sorrow will turn into joy.
When a woman is in travail she has sorrow,
because her Hour has come;
but when she is delivered of the child,
she no longer remembers the anguish,
for joy that a child is born into the world.
So you have sorrow now,
but I will see you again and your hearts will rejoice' (John 16¹⁹⁻²²).

It is significant that this quotation comes from the Fourth Gospel, whose thought our author echoes so closely. So too does the intimate connection between the crucifixion and the glorification of Christ—the child is no sooner 'born' than he is caught up to the throne of God. The crucifixion is not to be seen as an end in itself; it is the birth pangs of a new creation. Nor did the suffering it involved merely cease and give way to joy; it was the indispensable condition of that joy. The people

* Ch. 17.   † Ch. 21.   ‡ See especially 7⁴⁻⁸.

of God has to undergo these birth pangs in order to have a Messiah at all.

It is precisely in this event that the Dragon is cheated of his prey and so defeated. In this too our author remains true to the thought of the Fourth Gospel, where there is no reference to any conflict with Satan (as there is in Matthew, Mark and Luke —the temptation, the curing of numerous demoniacs) until the hour of Christ's passion. That is the final issue between God and Satan, the time when the prince of this world is cast out (John 12[31]). So it is here. The scene of Genesis 3 is, as it were, being repeated, and corrected, so that the people of God may again have access to the Tree of Life in Paradise. The Woman is again face to face with the Serpent,* again has to deliver in anguish, again declares her enmity with him, but now defeats him. And if he is already described as having ten horns and seven crowned heads, this is to prepare us for the later description of Rome,† which at the time of writing was the incarnation of the power of evil.

The defeat of Satan is emphasized in the paragraph which describes Michael and his angels casting him down from heaven to earth. We should not be too quick to identify this with that fall of the wicked angels which we place at the beginning of history. The symbolism has again been borrowed from the Jewish apocalyptic writings, where Michael is the protector of Israel who is to vanquish the enemy of God's People at the end of history.‡ What John is saying is that this victory of the End

---

* The Serpent or Dragon was already familiar in oriental mythology under the name of Rahab or Leviathan as the symbol of chaos. The symbolism was adopted by the Israelites to express their faith in a God who produced the ordered creation out of a chaos which constantly threatens to re-engulf it (see Gen. 1, Job 9[13], 26[12], Ps. 74[13], 89[10], Isa. 51[9]). This symbolism lies behind the portrayal of Satan as a dragon or serpent in this chapter as in Gen. 3, though this latter has also been influenced by the Canaanite cult of the serpent-god of fertility.

† See on 13[1] and 17[3].

‡ 'His tail swept down the stars of heaven' is a quotation from Dan. 8[10] of the monstrous force of this enemy of the light; 'There was no longer any place for them in heaven' is taken from Dan. 2[35] of the Kingdom of God replacing the kingdoms of this world.

Times took place in the mystical birth of the Messiah. Christ's death and resurrection not only cheated Satan of his prey, but dethroned him. If he continues to roam the earth and inflict harm, it is only for a short while. In essence he has been defeated.

Meanwhile the Woman also continues on earth, to suffer the repeated onslaught of the Dragon and to dwell in the wilderness for three and a half years. The time element has already been explained above in reference to ch. 11—it is 'persecution time'. The wilderness has the same meaning: it is the situation of hardship through which the people of God (or their representatives) have to pass before they can possess the Kingdom. This meaning was first given it in the Exodus, where forty years of desert existence stood between Israel and the Land promised them by God. But the 'desert theme' had been repeated many times since, in the history of David (1 Sam. 21ff. and 2 Sam. 15ff.), of Elijah (1 Ki. 17), of the Babylonian exiles (Isa. 40ff.), of the Maccabee martyrs (1 Macc. 2[28ff.]), of John the Baptist (Matt. 3[1]), and even of Christ himself (Matt. 4[1]). The Church cannot avoid traversing a similar desert before possessing the fullness of the Kingdom. Between the first and second coming of Christ, it is her destiny to suffer, and she is given the Eucharist during this intermediary stage so that she may have the strength to bear it. If she escapes the direct attack of Satan in one quarter, she will certainly meet him face to face in another. Verses 15-18 seem to refer to Rome's unexpected failure to engulf the Church in its siege of Jerusalem in the year 70, and to its turning in fury on 'the rest of the Woman's offspring' on the sea shore—the Christian communities in the coastlands of Asia Minor, for whom John is writing.

What this first tableau has shown us, therefore, is the people of God in all its magnificence. It was able to give birth to its Messiah only through suffering and pain: the crucifixion was necessary. Yet that birth was itself a victory over Satan: Christ is raised to glory, Satan is wrenched from his throne, and even the Christians of Jerusalem escape from his clutches. If he continues to persecute Christians elsewhere, this is only the necessary prelude to their own glorification.

This does not mean that the chapter has no reference to our Lady at all. If in St John's Gospel Mary, who figures only twice, is in both instances called 'The Woman'* that is to say, the person in whom the Old Testament Israel was finally summed up, then we may presume that she is not absent from this text either. We do right to suppose that our author must have had Mary somewhere in mind when he speaks of the mother of the Messiah. Mary is the prototype of the Church. At Calvary it was she who alone bore witness to her faith in Christ when the rest had fled. That anguish of hers bore fruit: it was there that she became the mother of all those 'whom Jesus loved' (John 19[26–27]). The birth of God's people could not be effected without Calvary. But those birthpangs produced not only Christ, but also the Christian community. And the mother of this birth was both the Church and Mary. The two are inseparable.

2. The Beast

The second of these three tableaux turns our attention from the Dragon-Serpent to the Beast, which is the form in which it arrives from overseas to the coast of Asia Minor.

> **13** [1]And I saw a beast rising out of the sea, with ten horns and seven heads, with ten diadems upon its horns and a blasphemous name upon its heads. [2]And the beast that I saw was like a leopard, its feet were like a bear's, and its mouth was like a lion's mouth. And to it the dragon gave his power and his throne and great authority. [3]One of its heads seemed to have a mortal wound, but its mortal wound was healed, and the whole earth followed the beast with wonder. [4]Men worshipped the dragon for he had given his authority to the beast, and they worshipped the beast, saying, 'Who is like the beast, and who can fight against it?'
>
> [5]And the beast was given a mouth uttering haughty and blasphemous words, and it was allowed to exercise authority for forty-two months; [6]it opened its mouth to utter blasphemies against

---

* See John 2[4] and 19[26]. St Luke sees Mary in a similar light, and in his first chapter applies to her the prophetical texts about Israel referred to above.

God, blaspheming his name and his dwelling, that is, those who dwell in heaven. ⁷Also it was allowed to make war on the saints and to conquer them. And authority was given it over every tribe and people and tongue and nation, ⁸and all who dwell on earth will worship it, every one whose name has not been written before the foundation of the world in the book of life of the Lamb that was slain. ⁹If anyone has an ear, let him hear:

¹⁰If anyone is to be taken captive,
    to captivity he goes;
if anyone slays with the sword,
    with the sword must he be slain.

Here is a call for the endurance and faith of the saints.

The text offers another example of how impossible it is to visualize these visions—how does one fit ten crowns on seven heads, or make those heads speak with one mouth? They have to be translated immediately into their intellectual equivalents if their meaning is to be seized. John has again gone to the book of Daniel and fused into one unimaginable monster the four beasts which had there symbolized the ferocity of succeeding pagan empires.* At the time of writing that paganism had been inherited by the Roman Empire, with its blasphemous claim that divine honour be paid to it,† and indeed ch. 17 will make this quite explicit. It is to this that Satan has given all his apparently irresistible power and his claim to the worship of the nations.

John sees the Roman Empire best represented by its two greatest persecutors—Nero, at whose death in 68 it had seemed to be doomed to dissolution ('a mortal wound'), and Domitian, the *Nero-redivivus*‡ upon whose succession in 81 it had most

---

* See Dan. 7.

† See the introductory chapter, and on 4¹¹. 'Who is like the beast?' is, of course, a parody of the phrase 'Who is like God?' (Mi-cha-El), which proclaims the uniqueness of God.

‡ Reference has already been made under 9¹¹ to the popular expectations of Nero's return after death. The phenomenon has continued to recur throughout history: for centuries after his death Barbarossa was reputed to be living in a cave near Salamanca; today, a full twenty years after the end of World War II, there are still legends of Hitler's survival in South America. But even apart from the legend, Domitian was another Nero, 'a bald version' Juvenal called him.

unexpectedly revived. It is this 'death and resurrection', says John, that has earned for Rome the adulation of the world, and, for the Christians who refused it, a lifetime (the 'three and a half years' of the Church's existence on earth) of persecution. His last verse is a quotation from Jerem. 15² of the inevitability of punishment for such persecutors.* It is meant as a message to inspire courage in those who have only exile and death to look forward to in this life, but who know that their names are written in the book of life.†

But even this Beast does not yet represent the full horror of what John has to convey. An incarnation of the previous chapter's Dragon, it is itself incarnated in another beast:

> 13 ¹¹Then I saw another beast which rose out of the earth; it had two horns like a lamb and it spoke like a dragon. ¹²It exercises all the authority of the first beast in its presence, and makes the earth and its inhabitants worship the first beast, whose mortal wound was healed. ¹³It works great signs, even making fire come down from heaven to earth in the sight of men; ¹⁴and by the signs which it is allowed to work in the presence of the beast, it deceives those who dwell on earth, bidding them make an image for the beast which was wounded by the sword and yet lived; ¹⁵and it was allowed to give breath to the image of the beast so that the image of the beast should even speak, and to cause those who will not worship the image of the beast to be slain. ¹⁶Also it causes all, both small and great, both rich and poor, both free and slave, to be marked on the right hand or the forehead, ¹⁷so that no one can buy or sell unless he has the mark, that is, the name of the beast or the number of its name. ¹⁸This calls for wisdom: let him who has understanding reckon the number of the beast, for it is a human number, its number is six hundred and sixty-six.

This Prophet of the Beast,‡ reminds us immediately of the false prophets who, as Christ warned his disciples, would come to them as wolves in sheep's clothing (Matt. 7¹⁵), comes not

---

* The fact that it is a quotation makes the alternative interpretation—that it is a Christian's duty to offer no resistance—unlikely.

† The parallel phrase in 17⁸ indicates that the text has correctly transposed the words 'before the foundation of the world.' Older versions have misleadingly connected them with 'the Lamb that was slain', and made of them a reference to the eternity of Christ's sacrifice.

‡ As it is called from 16¹³ onwards, to prevent confusion with *the* Beast.

from overseas like the Beast, but from the mainland. His task is to ensure the worship of the Beast, whose images it causes to breathe and to speak. Is this merely a vivid statement of the fact that the respect demanded for the imperial statues was like that demanded for the emperor himself, or have we a reference to the kind of conjuring tricks which, as we know, were practised in other eastern religions to impress the simple-minded? In either case we are here clearly dealing with the official Imperial Cult, which in Asia Minor was powerful enough to ostracize and even outlaw all those who refused to follow its dictates.* It had made of religion a state—almost a world—monopoly, and succeeded in completing the unholy trinity—a Dragon which sat enthroned in heaven, a Beast which is its incarnation and undergoes a death and resurrection, and a Prophet who proceeds from both and works miracles to inspire faith in them —which formed such a blasphemous parody of the God whom the Christian reader worshipped. He must resist to death the social, political and psychological pressures put on him to give divine honour to anything merely *human*, even though its name be as awe-inspiring as that to which a clue is given in the last verse of the chapter.

The 'name' has been variously interpreted. Indeed, given the fact that until the Arab invention of numerals all numbers were written in alphabetic letters, an endless number of combinations of letters can be made to provide the figure 666. In Hebrew and Greek in particular, where each letter had a numerical value, any word could be represented by a number simply by adding up those values, and this was in fact frequently done between those who wanted to share a secret.† The secret between John and his readers is not ours to share—he deliberately mentions that they need their wits about them at this point—but we can make a reasonably accurate guess at it. From the sibylline

* The mark of 13¹⁶ is to be taken no more literally than the mark of Christians in 7³.

† Martindale, *op. cit.* p. 102, quotes the delightful inscription still to be seen on a wall in Pompeii: 'I love the girl who adds up to 545.' Presumably both he and she knew who was meant, but no one else did.

oracles it is clear that Christians were already familiar with the fact that Christ's name in Greek (*Iesous*) could be added up to 888, a number which transcends the perfection of 777 throughout. The name of Nero written in Hebrew (*Nrwn Qsr*) is a laughable travesty of it, because it just misses that perfection throughout. It adds up to 666.*

The second tableau has therefore shown us, in a rich profusion of imagery, the Roman Empire in all its terrifying might. Embodied first in the great persecutor Nero, and then in the Nero-to-the-life that Domitian was, it made demands which simply could not be met by the Christians of the first century, who were unable to see in it anything else but a modern incarnation of the Satan who had tried to make away with Christ. It would be just as unsuccessful against them. John assures them of this by contrasting the 'world-church' of these ferocious beasts with the community dedicated to the Lamb:

14 ¹Then I looked, and lo, on Mount Zion stood the Lamb and with him a hundred and forty-four thousand who had his name and his Father's name written on their foreheads. ²And I heard a voice from heaven like the sound of many waters and like the sound of loud thunder; and the voice I heard was like the sound of harpers playing on their harps, ³and they sing a new song before the throne and before the four living creatures and before the elders. No one could learn that song except the hundred and forty-four thousand who had been redeemed from the earth. ⁴It is these who have not defiled themselves with women, for they are chaste; it is these who follow the Lamb wherever he goes; these have been redeemed from mankind as first fruits for God and the Lamb, ⁵and in their mouth no lie was found, for they are spotless.

* This is the explanation on which most scholars have agreed. Other alternatives that have been suggested, where they are serious—the Hebrew for Trajan, the Greek for the Latin Kingdom, the Latin numerals in the name DIOCLES AVGVSTVS (Diocletian)—all carry rather less probability, especially since the name of Nero (spelt without the final N which has a value of 50) alone accounts for the alternative reading in some manuscripts of the number as 616. Of course, there are many suggestions which cannot be taken seriously. The Seventh Day Adventists used to express their antipapalism by noting that the Latin numerals in the title VICARIVS FILII DEI add up to 666. During World War II it was discovered that, if 600 were added to the total, Hitler's name also gave the same result . . .

The numbers have already been used in 7⁴: here, as there, they represent the new Israel, the Christian Church in all its completeness and immensity; here, as there, they are already at peace with Christ in the new Jerusalem, even though under another aspect they are persecuted and hounded to death by the Beast. The desert into which they have followed Christ their leader* is both the place of trial and martyrdom, and the place of espousal to Christ. In other words, it is not only of consecrated virgins that John is speaking, but of all Christians. All Christians have to share in some sense in the life of virginity that is lived in heaven 'where they neither marry nor are given in marriage',† just as they have to share in some sense in the martydom by which alone they can bear witness to Christ before a world that is opposed to him. Without it they cannot form part of the new creation, or sing the new song‡ which marks their definitive exodus into the Kingdom of God.

3. The Judgment

The final tableau is a natural sequel to those that have preceded. The first has presented Satan's attempt to strangle Christianity at birth, and the second his commission to the Roman Empire to continue to wage his battle for him. Both have been filled with assurances that their efforts will fail. What remains except to describe God's judgment upon them both? The opening verses emphasize the finality of the scene.

14 ⁶Then I saw another angel flying in midheaven, with an eternal gospel to proclaim to those who dwell on earth, to every nation and

---

* See Jerem. 2²: Thus says the Lord,
        I remember the devotion of your youth,
        your love as a bride,
        how you followed me in the wilderness.

   † Matt. 22³⁰. St Paul had spoken of his Corinthian converts, married and unmarried, as 'virgins' in the same sense: see 2 Cor. 11².

   ‡ See on 5⁹ above.

tribe and tongue and people; ⁷and he said with a loud voice, 'Fear God and give him glory, for the hour of his judgment has come; and worship him who made heaven and earth, the sea and the fountains of water.'

⁸Another angel, a second, followed, saying, 'Fallen, fallen is Babylon the great, she who made all nations drink the wine of her impure passion.'

⁹And another angel, a third, followed, saying with a loud voice, 'If anyone worships the beast and its image, and receives a mark on his forehead or on his hand, ¹⁰he also shall drink the wine of God's wrath, poured unmixed into the cup of his anger, and he shall be tormented with fire and brimstone in the presence of the holy angels and in the presence of the Lamb. ¹¹And the smoke of their torment goes up for ever and ever; and they have no rest, day or night, these worshippers of the beast and its image, and whoever receives the mark of its name.'

¹²Here is a call for the endurance of the saints, those who keep the commandments of God and the faith of Jesus.

¹³And I heard a voice from heaven saying, 'Write this: Blessed are the dead who die in the Lord henceforth.' 'Blessed indeed,' says the Spirit, 'that they may rest from their labours, for their deeds follow them!'

¹⁴Then I looked, and lo, a white cloud, and seated on the cloud one like a son of man, with a golden crown on his head, and a sharp sickle in his hand. ¹⁵And another angel came out of the temple, calling with a loud voice to him who sat on the cloud, 'Put in your sickle, and reap, for the hour to reap has come, for the harvest of the earth is fully ripe.' ¹⁶So he who sat upon the cloud swung his sickle on the earth, and the earth was reaped.

¹⁷And another angel came out of the temple in heaven, and he too had a sharp sickle. ¹⁸Then another angel came out from the altar, the angel who has power over fire, and he called with a loud voice to him who had the sharp sickle, 'Put in your sickle, and gather the clusters of the vine of the earth, for its grapes are ripe.' ¹⁹So the angel swung his sickle on the earth and gathered the vintage of the earth, and threw it into the great wine press of the wrath of God; ²⁰and the wine press was trodden outside the city, and blood flowed from the wine press, as high as a horse's bridle, for one thousand six hundred stadia.

The Gospel, the good news proclaimed by each of the numerous angels of this vision is that in the midst of its apparent victory Rome has in reality already been defeated. The meaning of Christ's coming has not been appreciated by those who find this difficult to realize.* John gives it the name of 'Babylon', the great prototype of idolatry and paganism in the Old Testament, and quotes Isa. 21[9] of its fall in the conviction that the same fate awaits any government that sets itself up against God.† Those who connive with it have already been judged by God, and must inevitably suffer the fate reserved for Sodom and Gomorrah, and indeed for all the rubbish that was daily thrown out of Jerusalem to smoulder in the Ge-Henna or Valley of Hinnom.‡ It is this conviction that must uphold the Christian in his apparently unequal struggle against these powers. Even though they bring him to his death, they cannot lay hands on that eternal inheritance transcending death which he already possesses here and now in his union with the Christ who said: 'Come to me all who labour and are heavy burdened, and I will give you rest.'§

The judgment itself is described in terms of a Harvest, as it is frequently throughout Scripture.‖ The harvester is Christ himself, who is described as he was in 1[13], in his capacity as Son of Man, the heavenly figure scarcely distinct from God himself, who executes the judgment of God.¶ This he does, significantly,

* As those in the Middle Ages like Joachim de Floribus, who derived from the reference to 'an eternal gospel' the strange notion that our present gospel (the reign of Christ), like that of the Old Testament (the reign of the Father), is only a temporary one, and will give way to the eternal gospel of the future when the Holy Spirit's reign is established on earth. It is an essential part of Johannine thought that with the coming of Christ God had spoken his final word, and revealed his good news once and for all. There is no further revelation that he can give us.

† Ch. 17-18 will repeat the same text from Isaiah and develop the Babylon symbolism, not as a sequel to this scene (as if the quotation were some sort of 'prophetic perfect'), but simply as a repetition of it.

‡ Since the terms 'fire and brimstone' and 'smoke rising for ever' were borrowed from these two realities, and had in fact become classical as expressions of God's punishment of the wicked (see Isa. 34[8–10], 66[24]), they cannot be taken as a literal description of 'Gehenna' or hell.

§ Matt. 11[28]. The verse from the Apocalypse forms the lesson for Masses for the Dead.

‖ See Isa. 63[1–6], Joel 3[13], Matt. 13[30], 21[34], John 4[35], Gal. 6[7–9].

¶ Unless 'son of man' here refers to an angel. There would be reason for interpreting the title thus in this passage, since the ensuing grape-harvest is also reaped by an angel; the angels are the reapers in Matt. 13[39–41]. Certainly there are no grounds for distinguishing between a garnering of the just by Christ and a crushing of the wicked by an angel. Both harvests are a cutting down and a destruction.

in answer to the agonized cry of the martyrs at the altar from which the message to reap is given: 'How long before thou wilt avenge our blood?'* The scene is one of the bloodiest in the whole book, and it must again be pointed out that the terms are not to be taken literally. If God's judgment is to be expressed in terms of a battle, then blood and slaughter and war-horses are in order. But the battle is a metaphor borrowed from other apocalyptic writings, scriptural and otherwise.† Similarly metaphorical are the 1600 stadia or furlongs—they are simply the four corners of the earth squared to the tenth degree—and the location of the scene. The prophet Joel had envisaged the enemies of God, massed to attack the city where he dwelt, and overthrown before they had made the first assault. He had called their imaginary encampment the Valley of Jehoshaphat, but the word only means 'Of God's judgment.' (Joel 3²).

The song that is sung to greet this manifestation of God's justice‡ has already been suggested in the second tableau of this vision, and is an echo of the song that formed the finale to the very first vision in this series.§ All those who have resisted the pressure put on them to deny their true Lord have already completed their Exodus, and crossed the sea that divides heaven from earth.‖ Here and now they may take on their lips the words of victory sung by Moses and by Christ:

15 ²And I saw what appeared to be a sea of glass mingled with fire and those who had conquered the beast and its image and the number of its name, standing beside the sea of glass with harps of God in their hands. ³And they sing the song of Moses, the servant of God, and the song of the Lamb, saying,

'Great and wonderful are thy deeds,
O Lord God the Almighty!
Just and true are thy ways,
O King of the ages!

---

* See 5⁸, 6¹⁰, and the analysis given above of 8³⁻⁵.
† The Book of Henoch provided the gruesome detail of the horse's bridle.
‡ Mention has been made above that 15²⁻⁴ would seem to belong to this section rather than to the next.
§ See on 5⁹.   ‖ See on 4⁶.

> ⁴'Who shall not fear and glorify thy name, O Lord?
> For thou alone art holy.
> All nations shall come and worship thee,
> for thy judgments have been revealed.'*

The symbols used throughout these three tableaux—the Dragon, the Woman, the Beast, the Prophet, Babylon, the Lamb, the Harvest—will reappear in the chapters that follow. This does not mean that those chapters deal with events subsequent to those that have been described here. There is nothing that can be added to the Last Judgment, and this vision is meant to be as complete in itself as all the rest. John has again presented to us the persecution of his contemporaries under Domitian in the Asia Minor of the 90s, and shown it to be the climax of events which began with Satan's opposition to Christ in the 30s and Rome's attempt to annihilate the Jerusalem Christians in the 70s. The outcome of this present onslaught cannot be any more successful than those were. If John is able to give his readers such a vivid picture of Christ executing God's judgment on Rome and all its satellites, can they be in any doubt that this judgment has already started?

Babylon (chapters 17¹-19¹⁰)

With five of the seven sections into which John divides his 'revelation' behind us, we may admit that the Apocalypse is indeed a complicated book, but perhaps not so complicated as some think. It does not (as people say) go on and on and on. It keeps starting again from the beginning to say the same thing. Each of these sections has been entirely parallel to the others. It is not seven different sequences we are trying to grasp but only one, though it is expressed in seven different ways.

Some of these sections, as we have seen, are presented as a totality of seven in themselves (the seven seals, the seven trumpets, the seven bowls of wrath). But the rest are in looser form.

---

* The text is again a brilliant mosaic of Old Testament texts. See Exod. 15¹⁻², Ps. 92⁶, 98¹, 145¹⁷, Deut. 32⁴, Jerem. 10⁷, Ps. 86⁹⁻¹⁰, 72¹¹, 98².

Sometimes there has been only one central theme, which has slowly been opened out (The Lamb). Sometimes a number of tableaux have been presented in sequence to each other (the Serpent). Sometimes, finally, a number of tableaux are simply placed alongside each other, in parallel, but with no apparent sequence between them.* It is in the loosest of shapes that John's present statement of the theme is proposed, as the next will also be.

1. The Harlot and the Beast

The first tableau in this section sets forth the fall of Rome. This had already been the content of the last tableau of the section just dealt with (14⁶ᶠᶠ·) and of the fifth and seventh bowls of wrath in ch. 16. The theme is repeated here for the third time.

17 ¹Then one of the seven angels who had the seven bowls came and said to me, 'Come, I will show you the judgment of the great harlot who is seated upon many waters, ²with whom the kings of the earth have committed fornication, and with the wine of whose fornication the dwellers on earth have become drunk.' ³And he carried me away in the Spirit into a wilderness, and I saw a woman sitting on a scarlet beast which was full of blasphemous names, and it had seven heads and ten horns. ⁴The woman was arrayed in purple and scarlet, and bedecked with gold and jewels and pearls, holding in her hand a golden cup full of abominations and the impurities of her fornication; ⁵and on her forehead was written a name of mystery: 'Babylon the great, mother of harlots and of earth's abominations.' ⁶And I saw the woman, drunk with the blood of the saints and the blood of the martyrs of Jesus.

When I saw her I marvelled greatly. ⁷But the angel said to me, 'Why marvel? I will tell you the mystery of the woman, and of the beast with seven heads and ten horns that carries her. ⁸The beast that you saw was, and is not, and is to ascend from the bottomless pit and go to perdition; and the dwellers on earth whose names have

---

* Why not, then, count these tableaux as complete entities in themselves like each of the preceding sections, to give a total of eleven statements of the theme instead of seven? Because from the book's emphasis on the number seven it is not unreasonable to presume that its author planned this central portion of it in seven parts, and that these last six tableaux must therefore probably be considered as two groups of three. In actual fact, as will be seen, the connexion between each set of tableaux is sufficient to give them some sort of unity.

not been written in the book of life from the foundation of the
world, will marvel to behold the beast, because it was and is not and
is to come. [9]This calls for a mind with wisdom: the seven heads are
seven hills on which the woman is seated; [10]they are also seven
kings, five of whom have fallen, one is, the other has yet to come,
and when he comes he must remain only a little while. [11]As for the
beast that was and is not, it is an eighth but it belongs to the seven,
and it goes to perdition.

The scene takes place in the wilderness, the haunt of unclean
beasts, and the place where God's people must undergo trial.
There our attention is first focused on the Harlot. The imagery
is borrowed from the books of Isaiah and Jeremiah, which had
already described Tyre and Babylon as harlots,* the prototypes
of idolatry, that unfaithfulness to God which the prophets had
frequently called spiritual prostitution. The readers would
already be familiar with the notion of Rome as a reincarnation
of Babylon;† the added mockery of Rome's wealth and international influence in the flamboyant terms of a contemporary
prostitute‡ would be readily appreciated by those who were
unable to accept its favours and had suffered under its imper-
ialist pretensions.

The Beast on which Rome is enthroned is not so easy to
interpret. Basically, as we have seen, it is the Roman Empire—
its seven heads, we are explicitly told, represent Rome's famous
seven hills—with its demand for worship; its 'was and is not and
is to come' is a blasphemous claim to share God's own eternity,
the cause of the world's adulation. But John is not satisfied with
one level of symbolism. He wishes again to delight his readers
with an apparent riddle, and introduces it with the same rubric
with which he had underlined the mystical number of 13[8]. The
seven heads, he says, also stand for seven kings or emperors, of

---

* Isa. 23[16], 47[9], Jerem. 50-51. The description 'seated upon many waters'
comes from the latter passage, a reference to Babylon's position in the fertile
valley of the Tigris and Euphrates.

† See 1 Peter 5[13].

‡ Roman law required prostitutes to carry tickets with their names on
(verse 5), and 'gilding with gold' (the literal translation of verse 4) was not
unknown as a method of advertisement.

whom five are already in the past. These his readers would recognize as:

Augustus 27 B.C.-A.D. 14
Tiberius A.D. 14-37
Caligula A.D. 37-41
Claudius A.D. 41-54
Nero A.D. 54-68

The sixth, in the present, would therefore presumably be the army general Vespasian who succeeded to the throne after a year of bitter struggle for power in 69. Though they were reading it in the 90s, they were to imagine the vision as being written under Vespasian in the 70s: he is the one who 'is'. In the seventh, who is to rule for a short time only, they could not fail to see Titus, the short-lived son of Vespasian who held the throne for little more than a year between 79 and 81. And in the eighth, who is as it were the Beast all over again, they would recognize their own contemporary Domitian, who could be called one of the seven because he was in effect another Nero.

The fake perspective from which this, like so many other apocalypses, was written has complicated this picture. The author is taking a fictional standpoint in the 70s so that he can present the 80s and 90s as still being in the future.* But basically it is the picture already presented to us in ch. 13. Here, as there, the Beast is the Roman Empire, with its hideous parody of Christ's death and resurrection in its apparent dissolution after Nero's death ('it was and is not') and its remarkable revival under that second Nero, Domitian. Here, as there, the Beast has therefore to do duty for three distinct figures, the Empire and the two emperors who so successfully summed up all its evil. Here, as there, the issue is further complicated by the incorporation of the legend that Nero was still alive somewhere in the vassal states of the East, and would return from beyond the Euphrates at the head of a Parthian

* See above, pp. 12–16.

army to destroy the city over which he had once ruled.* This
is the gist of the closing verses of this chapter:

> **17** [12]And the ten horns that you saw are ten kings who have not yet
> received royal power, but they are to receive authority as kings for
> one hour, together with the beast. [13]These are of one mind and
> give over their power and authority to the beast; [14]they will make
> war on the Lamb, and the Lamb will conquer them, for he is Lord
> of lords and King of kings, and those with him are called and
> chosen and faithful.
>
> [15]And he said to me, 'The waters that you saw, where the harlot
> is seated, are peoples and multitudes and nations and tongues.
> [16]And the ten horns that you saw, they and the beast will hate the
> harlot; they will make her desolate and naked, and devour her flesh
> and burn her up with fire, [17]for God has put it into their hearts to
> carry out his purpose by being of one mind and giving over their
> royal power to the beast, until the words of God shall be fulfilled.
> [18]And the woman that you saw is the great city which has dominion
> over the kings of the earth.'

As the last words of the tableau indicate, for all the intricate
symbolism that has gone into the making of the Beast, the
emphasis is not on it but on the city of Rome that rides on its
back. It is she whose destruction is here envisaged. The second
tableau will deal with exactly the same thing.

2. The Doom of Rome

If in general John has had no qualms about borrowing the
materials with which to compose his visions, here he has
excelled himself. The whole chapter is nothing but an anthology
of the songs with which the Old Testament prophets had
already greeted the falls of Nineveh (Nahum 3[4]), Tyre (Isa. 23,
Ezek. 26-28), Edom (Isa. 34[8-14]), Jerusalem itself (Jerem. 7[34],
16[9], 25[10]), and especially Babylon (Isa. 13[20-22], 21[9], 44[23], 47-48,
52[11], Jerem. 25[27], 50-51, Ps. 137[8]). Such an anthology requires
no commentary. It is a generic, and in many ways ironic,
condemnation of godlessness, of any civilization which tries
to be self-sufficient and to leave God out of its reckoning. The
fact that history had witnessed the successive dooms of these

---

* See again on 9[11] and 13[3].

civilizations must be the readers' security that the Rome under which he suffers is also divinely doomed.

18 [1]After this I saw another angel coming down from heaven, having great authority; and the earth was made bright with his splendour. [2]And he called out with a mighty voice,

'Fallen, fallen is Babylon the great!
It has become a dwelling place of demons,
a haunt of every foul spirit,
a haunt of every foul and hateful bird;
[3]for all nations have drunk the wine of her impure passion,
and the kings of the earth have committed fornication with her,
and the merchants of the earth have grown rich
with the wealth of her wantonness.'

[4]Then I heard another voice from heaven saying,

'Come out of her, my people,
lest you take part in her sins,
lest you share in her plagues;
[5]for her sins are heaped high as heaven,
and God has remembered her iniquities.
[6]Render to her as she herself has rendered,
and repay her double for her deeds;
mix a double draught for her in the cup she mixed.
[7]As she glorified herself and played the wanton,
so give her a like measure of torment and mourning.
Since in her heart she says, "A queen I sit,
I am no widow, mourning I shall never see",
[8]so shall her plagues come in a single day,
pestilence and mourning and famine,
and she shall be burned with fire;
for mighty is the Lord God who judges her.'

[9]And the kings of the earth, who committed fornication and were wanton with her, will weep and wail over her when they see the smoke of her burning; [10]they will stand far off, in fear of her torment, and say,

'Alas! alas! thou great city,
thou mighty city, Babylon!
In one hour has thy judgment come.'

[11]And the merchants of the earth weep and mourn for her, since no one buys their cargo any more, [12]cargo of gold, silver, jewels and pearls, fine linen, purple, silk and scarlet, all kinds of scented wood, all articles of ivory, all articles of costly wood, bronze, iron and marble, [13]cinnamon, spice, incense, myrrh, frankincense, wine, oil,

fine flour and wheat, cattle and sheep, horses and chariots, and slaves, that is, human souls.

> [14]'The fruit for which thy soul longed has gone from thee,
> and all thy dainties and thy splendour are lost to thee,
> never to be found again!'

[15]The merchants of these wares, who gained wealth from her, will stand far off, in fear of her torment, weeping and mourning aloud,

> [16]'Alas, alas, for the great city
> that was clothed in fine linen, in purple and scarlet,
> bedecked with gold, with jewels and with pearls!
> [17]In one hour all this wealth has been laid waste.'

And all shipmasters and seafaring men, sailors and all whose trade is on the sea, stood far off [18]and cried out as they saw the smoke of her burning,

> 'What city was like the great city?'

[19]And they threw dust on their heads, as they wept and mourned, crying out,

> 'Alas, alas, for the great city
> where all who had ships at sea grew rich by her wealth!
> [20]Rejoice over her, O heaven,
> O saints and apostles and prophets,
> for God has given judgment for you against her!'

[21]Then a mighty angel took up a stone like a great millstone and threw it into the sea, saying,

> 'So shall Babylon the great city be thrown down with violence
> and shall be found no more;
> [22]and the sound of harpers and minstrels,
> of flute players and trumpeters,
> shall be heard in thee no more,
> and a craftsman of any craft
> shall be found in thee no more,
> and the sound of the millstone
> shall be heard in thee no more;
> [23]and the light of a lamp
> shall shine in thee no more;
> and the voice of bridegroom and bride
> shall be heard in thee no more;
> for thy merchants were the great men of the earth,
> and all nations were deceived by thy sorcery.
> [24]And in her was found the blood of prophets and of saints,
> and of all who have been slain on earth.'

3. The Song of the Redeemed

Parallel with that doleful song of mourning, and in contrast with it, the last of these three tableaux presents the song of triumph that bursts forth from the lips of those for whom this fall of Rome can only spell joy. The song has already been sung in 5^9, 7^{10}, 14^3 and 15^3, and phrases from it are echoed here.

19 ¹After this I heard what seemed to be the mighty voice of a great multitude in heaven, crying,

'Hallelujah! Salvation and glory and power belong to our God,
²for his judgments are true and just;
he has judged the great harlot
who corrupted the earth with her fornication,
and he has avenged on her the blood of his servants.'

³Once more they cried,

'Hallelujah! The smoke from her goes up for ever and ever.'

⁴And the twenty-four elders and the four living creatures fell down and worshipped God who is seated on the throne, saying, 'Amen. Hallelujah!' ⁵And from the throne came a voice crying,

'Praise our God, all you his servants,
you who fear him, small and great.'

⁶Then I heard what seemed to be the voice of a great multitude, like the sound of many waters and like the sound of many thunder-peals, crying,

'Hallelujah! For the Lord our God the Almighty reigns.
⁷Let us rejoice and exult and give him the glory,
for the marriage of the Lamb has come,
and his Bride has made herself ready;
⁸it was granted to her to be clothed with fine linen,
bright and pure'—

for the fine linen is the righteous deeds of the saints.
⁹And the angel said to me, 'Write this: Blessed are those who are invited to the marriage supper of the Lamb.' And he said to me, 'These are true words of God.'

The closing verses again emphasize the definitive character of this scene. When the kingdom has come, nothing more can be added. When the marriage covenant between God and mankind has been consummated, God's plans are complete. What is to follow can only be a repetition of this, not a sequel.* So aware of this is the author that he portrays himself as stunned by this vision of the End:

> **19** **¹⁰**Then I fell down at his (the angel's) feet to worship him, but he said to me, 'You must not do that! I am a fellow servant with you and your brethren who hold the testimony of Jesus. Worship God.' For the testimony of Jesus is the spirit of prophecy.

We have already met, in the introduction, the first century misinterpretation of Christianity which advocated the worship of angels. The angel's disclaimer here is probably a piece of polemic inspired by this Gnostic background: angels are nothing but servants of the one true God; their task, like that of any Christian, can only be to bear witness to Christ. But the polemic is also a fine piece of drama to mark the conclusion of the theme.

The complete theme has therefore been repeated for the sixth time, even if in a looser form. For the first century Christian, Rome sums up the whole power of evil mobilized against the Church. When that fails God's Kingdom comes, and there is nothing more that can be said. To stress the inevitability of this, John has put the perspective back ten years into the reign of Vespasian. If the reader envisages the fall of Rome and the establishment of God's Kingdom as still lying in the future, he must be assured that they will follow as surely as Domitian followed Vespasian. If he has seen that part of this 'prophecy' fulfilled, he can remain in no doubt about the rest.

The Defeat of Evil (chapters 19¹¹-22⁵)

The final statement of the theme begins, as all the others have done, at the beginning. The very technique used—of the opening of the heavens to reveal what has so far been the secret of God—has proved so effective before† that John does not hesitate to use it again. The vision that meets his eyes is again

---

* The marriage theme is to be developed in the last tableau of the next series.
† See 4¹, 11¹⁹, 15⁵.

described in three scenes. As in the previous section, they are parallel rather than in sequence to each other.

1. The Horseman

19 [11]Then I saw heaven opened, and behold, a white horse! He who sat upon it is called Faithful and True, and in righteousness he judges and makes war. [12]His eyes are like a flame of fire, and on his head are many diadems; and he has a name inscribed which no one knows but himself. [13]He is clad in a robe dipped in blood and the name by which he is called is The Word of God. [14]And the armies of heaven, arrayed in fine linen, white and pure, followed him on white horses. [15]From his mouth issues a sharp sword with which to smite the nations, and he will rule them with a rod of iron; he will tread the wine press of the fury of the wrath of God the Almighty. [16]On his robe and on his thigh he has a name inscribed, King of kings and Lord of lords.

The horseman on a white horse is a symbol, as he was in 6^2, for conquest. This time he does not form part of a quartet but stands alone, and there can be no doubt that the portrait intended is that of Christ. As in 1^5, 3^7 and 3^{14} he is the living guarantee that God is faithful to his promises. As in 1^{14} and 2^{18} he is the all-knowing searcher of minds and hearts, and as in 1^{16} and 2^{12} the inescapable punisher of evil. As in 2^{27} and 12^4 he is, despite all appearances to the contrary, the dominating force in the world, and as in 1^5 bears the crown over all other rulers. He is, in short, the 'Word' of God,* the sum total of all that God ever had or ever will have to reveal to men. He is the assurance that the first century reader requires, that though the Lord to whom he is trying to remain true seems to the world's eyes— even at times to his own—to be an irrelevance, a figment to be

---

* It has already been pointed out that here the author shows himself to be of one mind with the writers of the Gospel and epistles of St John, who is otherwise alone in using this title of Christ. There seems at first sight to be some inconsistency in specifying as unknowable a name which is then given not only as 'Word of God' but also as 'Faithful and True' and 'King of kings and Lord of lords', the latter written on the only part of his robe that contains no folds, as on an equestrian statue. But these names are descriptive rather than definitive. The emphasis would seem to remain on the name as a revelation of a person's inner nature, which in the case of Christ remains as inaccessible a mystery as God's own.

suppressed or, worse, ignored, he is in reality the king-pin of the universe, and its fate lies entirely in his hands.

This is emphasized when the scene is further opened out, and the followers of this divine Warrior are revealed drawn up in battle against the retinue of the Beast—the Roman Empire and its satellites.

> **19** [17]Then I saw an angel standing in the sun, and with a loud voice he called to all the birds that fly in midheaven, 'Come, gather for the great supper of God, [18]to eat the flesh of kings, the flesh of captains, the flesh of mighty men, the flesh of horses and their riders, and the flesh of all men, both free and slave, both small and great.' [19]And I saw the beast and the kings of the earth and their armies gathered to make war against him who sits on the horse and against his army. [20]And the beast was captured, and with it the false prophet who in its presence had worked the signs by which he deceived those who had received the mark of the beast and those who worshipped its image. These two were thrown alive into the lake of fire that burns with brimstone. [21]And the rest were slain by the sword of him who sits upon the horse, the sword that issues from his mouth; and all the birds were gorged with their flesh.

The imagery may not be to our taste; certainly this gruesome meal is something quite different to what the phrase 'The Lord's Supper' generally conjures up in our minds. But the terms are again borrowed ones: the picture of the cloak soaked in enemy blood comes from Isa. 63[1-6], and that of birds gorged on enemy flesh from Ezek. 39[17-20]. Not that this recognition of John's sources must empty his words of their meaning: even in its transposed sense we do well to remind ourselves that the service of God will always involve a warfare, and if need be bloodshed.* With God's enemies—and they are more often interior than exterior to us—there can be no compromise. Their end must be as bloody and definitive† as that of the Roman Empire and its adherents described here.

* The epistle to the Hebrews uses the thought to give renewed courage to its readers: 'In your struggle against sin you have not yet resisted to the point of shedding blood'—with the understanding—'but you may well have to' (Heb. 12[4]).

† The lake of fire has occurred in 14[10] as a symbol of eternal punishment. It will be used again in the same sense in 20[10] and 21[8].